W9-AYD-549

LONELY PLANET
ROAD TRIP

HUDSON
RIVER VALLEY

China Williams

Road Trip Hudson River Valley
1st edition – July 2004

Published by Lonely Planet Publications Pty Ltd
ABN 36 005 607 983

Australia	Head Office, Locked Bag 1, Footscray, Vic 3011
	☎ 03 8379 8000 fax 03 8379 8111
	📧 talk2us@lonelyplanet.com.au
USA	150 Linden St, Oakland, CA 94607
	☎ 510 893 8555 toll free 800 275 8555
	fax 510 893 8572
	📧 info@lonelyplanet.com
UK	72–82 Rosebery Avenue, London EC1R 4RW
	☎ 020 7841 9000 fax 020 7841 9001
	📧 go@lonelyplanet.co.uk
France	1 rue du Dahomey, 75011 Paris
	☎ 01 55 25 33 00 fax 01 55 25 33 01
	📧 bip@lonelyplanet.fr
	🖥 www.lonelyplanet.fr

This title was commissioned in Lonely Planet's Oakland
office and produced by: **Commissioning Editor** &
Project Manager Kathleen Munnelly
Series Designer & **Cover Designer** Candice Jacobus
Regional Publishing Manager David Zingarelli

Freelancers: Cartographer Bart Wright
Editor Emily Wolman **Indexer** Ken DellaPenta
Proofer Michele Posner

Cover photograph Old Chatham, New York,
Andre Jenny/Alamy Images. All images are copyright
of the photographers unless otherwise indicated.

ISBN 1 74059 573 4

Printed through The Bookmaker International Ltd.
Printed in China

CONTENTS

FROM THE PUBLISHER

AUTHOR

China Williams

Once her ship comes in, China will buy a Victorian fixer-upper in Kingston, New York, and open the nation's first pizza shop/flower nursery/record store. Until then, China hangs her globetrotting backpack in Portland, Maine, where she shares a sunny apartment with her husband, Matt.

Thanks to the region's great bookstore owners who talked art, jazz, local politics and good eats with me. Also thanks to the kind folks at Saugerties Lighthouse B&B, Peekskill Inn and Historic Hudson Valley for showering me with attention and brochures. Also many thanks to the awesome American historical figures who bestowed their intelligence and vision upon such a majestic landscape. Much kudos to the talented Lonely Planet team, including Kathleen Munnelly, Emily Wolman and Bart Wright. And final thanks to my husband who gallantly picks me up from the airport or drives me back to Vacationland.

SEND US YOUR FEEDBACK

We love to hear from travelers – your comments keep us on our toes and help make our books better. Our well-traveled team reads every word on what you loved or loathed about this book. Although we cannot reply individually to postal submissions, we always guarantee that your feedback goes straight to the appropriate authors, in time for the next edition – and the most useful submissions are rewarded with a free book. To send us your updates – and find out about LP events, newsletters and travel news – visit our award-winning website: 🖳 **www.lonelyplanet.com.**

Note: We may edit, reproduce and incorporate your comments in Lonely Planet products such as guidebooks, websites and digital products, so let us know if you don't want your comments reproduced or your name acknowledged. For a copy of our privacy policy visit 🖳 www.lonelyplanet.com/privacy.

HOW TO USE THIS BOOK

Opening hours for places listed in this book apply during summer, except where otherwise noted. When entry fees are not listed, sites are free (although some may request a small donation). Price gradings (eg $10/7/5) indicate admission for adults/students & seniors/children.

Text Symbols

☎	telephone	s	single rooms
🖳	Internet available	d	double rooms
☯	opening hours	ste	suites
Ⓟ	parking available	dm	dorm beds
🏊	swimming pool		

INTRODUCTION

From a riverbank along the Hudson, it's easy to imagine a New York of another era, when tall masted ships sailed a watery highway, and muddy lanes cut through small villages of dairy farms and regal manor houses. In the thick woods between, arching branches formed cathedral ceilings, squeezing sunlight into dappled patterns like monochromatic stained glass. This is the same recognizable landscape captured in the luminous paintings by the famous artists of the Hudson River school.

Long before these painters recorded the valley in oil, Henry Hudson sailed up the river, claiming the wilderness for his employers, the Dutch East India Company, in 1609. Proving not to be the Northwest Passage as he had hoped, the river valley nevertheless became an important link for the European fur trade. During the colonial period, Dutch and English farmers filtered into the area, pushing out the local Native American tribes, including the Mohicans and the Iroquois. Unique to New York State, the Dutch Colonial influence is still evident in the culture and architecture of this area.

In the mid-19th century, the Hudson River Valley was given its most enduring role in history. Rapid industrialization spread up the river to the newly opened Erie Canal, creating unprecedented wealth, immigration and disorder. Factories replaced farmland, cities eclipsed villages, and a new generation of artists rebelled against this modernization. Known as the Romantics, these artists embraced the wild beauty of the Hudson River Valley as a utopia untainted by the evils of the modern world. They sketched the dramatic forests, built retreats in concert with the landscape and wrote tall tales of the uninhabited woods. Once the railroad was extended up the eastern side of the valley, the wealthy industrialists joined in with their own version of escapism.

Even today, the Hudson River Valley still holds the promise of a simpler life far removed from the headaches of the modern world. The small hamlets and two-lane country roads not only survive, they even outnumber the suburban strip malls. Pick-your-own farms and produce stands connect urban refugees with the harvest cycle, and the numerous state parks, including the Catskill Mountains, give solitude to the over-stimulated. Thanks to the preservation of historic homes, the ideals of the Romantic age persist – human necessities can meet the landscape as a friend, not a foe.

Living museum, three-dimensional landscape painting, bucolic refuge – the Hudson River Valley is certainly all of these things. But it has another side as well: the influence of artists and former city-dwellers has made this area a cultured oasis of antiquarian bookstores, cutting-edge art galleries and haute cuisine restaurants. It is a stunning balance of rural and urban that every burned-out city-dweller dreams about.

The Hudson River Valley refers to the area south of Albany that follows the Hudson River and lies between the Catskill Mountains to the west and the Taconic highlands and the Connecticut state border to the east. For this book, the Hudson River Valley has been divided into three sections: the eastern bank, the western bank and the Taconic State Parkway.

GETTING THERE & AROUND

Route 9 is the principal scenic north-south road in the Hudson Valley, and it hugs the east side of the river for the most part; when it strays, Route 9D near Cold Spring and Route 9G near Rhinebeck continue the riverside route. On the west side of the river is **Route 9W**, which is more utilitarian than its eastern cousin. Also on the river's west side is the scenic **Palisades Interstate Parkway**, which begins in Ft Lee, NJ, and runs north through Harriman State Park and ends at Route 9W in Bear Mountain State Park.

The area farther east of the river is paralleled by the **Taconic State Parkway**, which connects the towns of Old Chatham, southeast of Albany, and Hawthorne, east of Sleepy Hollow.

To cover ground quickly, jump on east-west **I-287**, which runs into north-south **I-87** (the New York State Thruway – often called the 'Northway'). I-87 continues north into the Catskills region. For Thruway road conditions, call ☎ 800-847-8929.

If escaping from New York City, follow the Bronx River Parkway north to pick up the Taconic; the Deegan Expressway (I-87) or the Henry Hudson Parkway/Saw Mill River Parkway to pick up Route 9 around Tarrytown; or the George Washington Bridge across the Hudson River to the Palisades for Route 9W.

If departing from points in New England, follow the main east-west route of **I-84**. Once you cross the state line, you can swing south via I-684 to the Saw Mill River Parkway to Route 9 around Tarrytown and Sleepy Hollow. Other options are to follow I-84 all the way through to Route 9D around Beacon or to cross the river just north of Newburgh.

The closest major airports are in New York City and Albany. **La Guardia** (LGA; ☎ 718-533-3400), in northern Queens, services mostly domestic flights, including most northeastern cities and air shuttles to Boston and Washington, DC. **Newark International Airport** (EWR; ☎ 201-961-6000), in New Jersey, is the hub for Continental Airlines and is also used by international and domestic flights of all

↓
GETTING THERE & AROUND

Did You Know?

The Hudson River begins in the Adirondacks at Lake Tear-of-the-Cloud, atop Mt Marcy. It flows south over 300 miles to New York Bay, forming an estuary so large that Dutch navigator Henry Hudson mistook the river for the Northwest Passage, the coveted route to the Far East. Subject to tidal variations, the Hudson acts more like a fjord than a river.

major carriers. Another international airport is **John F Kennedy** (JFK; ☎718-244-4444), in southeastern Queens.

Albany International Airport (ALB; ☎518-869-9611; Albany-Shaker Rd) is in the town of Colonie, about 10 miles northwest of downtown Albany. Most major carriers serve the airport. A smaller regional option is **Stewart International Airport** (SWF; ☎845-564-7200; Route 17K), 2 miles west of Newburgh. It is served by several carriers, including **Delta** (☎800-354-9833), **Southeast Airlines** (☎800-359-7325), **American Eagle** (☎800-433-7300) and **US Airways Express** (☎800-428-4322).

Short Line/Coach USA Bus Co (☎800-631-8405; www.short linebus.com) offers the best service to the Hudson Valley, including West Point, Bear Mountain and Newburgh. They also offer day-trip packages that include a bus ride and taxi transfer to a particular attraction.

Amtrak (☎800-872-7245; www.amtrak.com) runs trains along the length of the eastern shore of the river, connecting Penn Station in New York City with Croton-on-Hudson, Poughkeepsie, Rhinecliff-Rhinebeck, Hudson and beyond to Albany and towns in the Adirondacks ($50-80 roundtrip). Some people do weekend trips to these towns and get around to far-flung sites by taxi.

Metro-North (☎212-532-4900, 800-638-7646; www.mta.info) operates the Hudson commuter line from Grand Central Station in New York City to east-bank towns such as Tarrytown, Ossining, Peekskill, Beacon and as far north as Poughkeepsie.

The best rental car rates are from the airports (in this case Albany, Newark and Newburgh).

ITINERARIES

THE CLASSIC: ONE TO TWO WEEKS

Paying homage to the venerable Hudson River is a noble vacation, especially for New York City–based travelers. For the true river connoisseur, tracing a loop up one side and down the other accommodates all the highlights.

For argument's sake, let's start with the eastern bank. Once you forge your way out of New York City, stop in at **Tarrytown** and **Sleepy Hollow** for two days. This is where Washington Irving built his quirky cottage of gables and gardens and where the Rockefellers cemented a dynasty. Follow Route 9 north to **Cold Spring**, an idyllic village within striking distance of Boscobel (a historic house museum with the best Hudson River view around) and Beacon's impressive modern art museum, Dia: Beacon. Give yourself a day or two here and then shoot up to **Hyde Park** to pay a visit to the national historic sites dedicated to Eleanor and Franklin Delano Roosevelt. Your understanding of their roles in 20th-century history will be greatly enhanced by visiting their comfortable, subdued residences. Before cruising into town, make a reservation at one of the Culinary Institute of America's student-run restaurants.

Full of food and history, you are ready for romantic **Rhinebeck**. Stroll its well-starched downtown, walk the same path by the Hudson River as Washington Irving did or visit a few pretty houses. **Hudson** is the next town on the eastern circuit and full of antiques, country drives and Olana, the lifesize landscape painting of Frederic Edwin Church.

Depending on your interests, you should hop over to the western bank for a tour of **West Point**, a visit to the outdoor sculpture garden of **Storm King Art Center**, a hike in **New Paltz** or just to hang out in **Woodstock**. At some point in your travels through the Hudson Valley, you should drive a portion of the **Taconic State Parkway**, eat at a railcar diner, and load up with fruits and veggies from a roadside market.

THE GREAT WEEKEND ESCAPE

If you limit yourself to one area mentioned above, you have created an instant weekend escape, but consider these other popular options. Keep in mind that only Cold Spring and Hudson are compact enough to allow for visitors to arrive by train and survive without a car, if they stick to the in-town attractions. Cabbing to outlying attractions can easily equal the cost of a day's car rental.

Romantic Cold Spring – Staying in a quaint B&B, antiquing and walking arm in arm; Cold Spring has few other distractions.

Antiquing in Hudson – In just a two-hour train ride, you are at the foot of one of the longest streets dedicated to antiques.

Getting Outdoors – Bear Mountain and Harriman State Park are so close to NYC that you can practically hear the subway. Lounging beside Lake Taghkanic is a great way to spend an Indian summer. To give the mountain bike a workout, head to New Paltz.

Festivals & Retreats – Build a vacation around one of the region's many special events, including Woodstock's film festival, Saugerties' jazz festival, or Halloween events in Tarrytown and Sleepy Hollow. Spiritual retreats (p51), from yoga to meditation, are offered throughout the valley and can be tailored to fit a work schedule.

HIGHLIGHTS

Best View of the Hudson River: The river hangs a sharp right into a shallow cove that laps at the feet of the landscaped grounds of **Boscobel** (p18). The effect is breathtaking, with the outstretched palm of the river framed by stooped trees and emerald lawn.

Proof That a Yard Is an Outdoor Canvas: From modern to antique, **Storm King Art Center** (p45), **Clermont Historic Site** (p31) and **Innisfree Garden** (p36) are all variations on the Hudson Valley's devotion to landscape art.

Two Good Reasons to Read Biographies: A truly modern couple, FDR and his wife Eleanor exemplified how compassion and diplomacy can mend a wounded country; find out more at the **FDR National Historic Site** (p21) and **Eleanor Roosevelt Historic Site** (p23).

Best Use of A Box Factory: A converted factory, **Dia: Beacon** (p20) has smuggled modern art out of the cramped galleries of Manhattan to give the pieces enough room to overwhelm the viewer.

Most Romantic Getaway: The cute Victorian village of **Cold Spring** (p19) is perfect for strolling along the Hudson, visiting nearby historic homes, perusing modern art galleries and dreaming of idyllic futures within commuting distance of the city.

Best Spicy Meal: In the artist colony of Tivoli, funky **Santa Fe Restaurant** (p29) gives credence to 'nuevo Mexican' cuisine.

Best Waterfall: The 260ft **Kaaterskill Falls** (p58) inspired generations of painters, including Thomas Cole, who immortalized the falls in his work *View of Kaaterskill Falls.*

EASTERN BANK

By the show of summer estates, the eastern bank might be erroneously named the most beautiful side of the Hudson River. More accurately, the eastern bank has a more beautiful view of the Catskill Mountains rising over the western bank.

The best route to the gateway village of Tarrytown is via the Henry Hudson Parkway to the wooded speedway of the Saw Mill River Parkway. The parkway feeds deliberately onto I-87 with a sharp exit for Route 9 right before the Tappan Zee Bridge. Rounding the exit ramp, you're delivered into the heart of Westchester County and Tarrytown just to the north.

TARRYTOWN & SLEEPY HOLLOW

Population: Tarrytown 11,000, Sleepy Hollow 9200; Map 2

Washington Irving once stated that Tarrytown got its name from the Dutch farm wives who complained that their husbands tarried a bit too long at the village tavern after selling their farm produce at the nearby markets. The more likely, but less appealing, linguistic explanation finds it a variation of the Dutch *tarwe*, meaning wheat.

Historic Tarrytown has the appearance of a quaint village but all the energy of a New York City suburb – people are constantly in a rush, and Route 9 through town is more congested than a winter head cold. Regardless, Tarrytown is the most convenient base for touring the largest concentrations of historic house museums along the river. The average person can probably stand oohing and aahing at two historic homes a day, so plan your trip accordingly. Thanks to the enduring legacy of the Headless Horseman, Halloween is celebrated here with great enthusiasm.

As a tourism campaign, the village of North Tarrytown decided that it might do better if it changed its name to Sleepy Hollow – and so it did. Look out for old maps that might bear the old North Tarrytown name.

SIGHTS & ACTIVITIES

SUNNYSIDE

☎ 914-591-8763; W Sunnyside Lane, 3 miles south of Tarrytown off Rte 9; adult/senior/child $9/8/5, grounds pass $4; ⊙10:30am-4pm Mon & Wed-Sun Apr-Oct, call for winter hours

Washington Irving, author of *The Legend of Sleepy Hollow*, described his Hudson Valley home as being 'made up of gable ends and full of angles and corners as an old cocked hat.' Even today, it's easy to imagine Irving staring into the deep forests and ravines and envisioning the Headless Horseman of Sleepy Hollow chasing poor Ichabod Crane. When Irving moved to Sunnyside, it was to combine the watery solitude of this sleepy

Kids' Stuff

Wondering what to do with the little 'uns? Try these on for size:
- **Bear Mountain State Park** (Palisades Parkway, p42) – hiking, swimming and a carousel
- **Catskill Game Farm** (Catskill, p59) – petting zoo with 2000 animals
- **FDR National Historic Site** (Hyde Park, p21) – an introduction to presidential history
- **Kaaterskill Falls** (near Catskill, p58) – a larger vertical drop than Niagara Falls
- **Museum of the Hudson Highlands** (Cornwall-on-Hudson, p45) – nature center and walking trails
- **Old Rhinebeck Aerodrome** (Rhinebeck, p28) – vintage airplane museum and air shows
- **Philipsburg Manor** (Tarrytown, p11) – a living history farm with real live animals
- **Pick-your-own farms** (p27) – good old-fashioned child labor
- **Sunnyside** (Tarrytown, p9) – special programs throughout the year, including some ghoulish Halloween events

hollow by the river with proximity to the bustling metropolis of New York City. Only 10 years after Irving built Sunnyside on a serene hillside, the railroad came up the river and could not be stopped, even by America's most famous author. Irving cursed the coal-burning steam engine as it passed his home, shaking the ground. He made a compromise of sorts by finally using the train to venture into New York City. Interestingly, this was the first home that Irving had ever owned, and he purchased it at the ripe old age of 53.

Visitors can see this cottage on a guided, one-hour tour. As the costumed tour guide will surely tell you, Irving's old Dutch cottage was 'cute, cozy, quiet and charming.' The age of Romanticism is greatly at work here, just as it worked on Irving's imagination. Like all Romantics, he found a divine spirit in nature. The formal English hedges are gone, replaced by a carefully designed 'natural' look. The climbing wisteria that Irving planted over a century ago still clings to the house. The house tour reveals how people of leisure spent time at home, took advantage of the daylight hours and often gathered 'round the piano in the evening.

LYNDHURST

☎ 914-631-4481; 635 S Broadway/Rte 9; adult/senior/student/child $10/9/4/free, grounds pass $4; ☉10am-5pm Tue-Sun Apr-Oct

This historic home, 1.6 miles south of Tarrytown's center, is a classic Gothic Revival mansion designed by the leading architect of the genre, Alexander Jackson Davis, in the 1830s. The home, which overlooks the Hudson, was built for the mayor of New York City, William Paulding. The landscaping – particularly the rose garden, containing more than 100 varieties arranged in a circular pattern around a gazing gazebo – is as spectacular as the building. A small map identifying most of the flora is available at the entrance gate when you drive in.

PHILIPSBURG MANOR
☎ 914-631-3992; N Broadway/Rte 9, 2 miles north of Tarrytown; adult/senior/child $9/8/5; ⏰10am-4pm Mon & Wed-Sun Apr-Oct

Has your child mastered all the barnyard animal noises but hasn't yet met the real McCoys? It is time to introduce the kids to farming, 17th-century-style, at this educational history museum. Like many wealthy Europeans, the Dutchman Frederick Philips was awarded a large tract of land here, on which he built a family home, a water-powered gristmill and a Dutch church. Visitors will see farm workers in period dress performing the chores of the day, from tending the vegetable garden to milking the cows. Cocky roosters strut across the grounds, and the yard cat, Scooter, makes friends with everyone. In the pasture, you might see a lounging cow beside a muddy stream shaded by a weeping willow – an inadvertent staging of a Hudson River School painting. Activities are geared toward kids of all ages, and special events, like sheep shearing, are tied to the agricultural calendar.

Philipsburg is also the starting point for tours to **Kykuit** (below).

OLD DUTCH CHURCH & SLEEPY HOLLOW CEMETERY
☎ 914-631-0081 church office; N Broadway/Rte 9; admission free;
⏰8am-4:30pm Mon-Sun

Across the road from Philipsburg Manor, this 1865 church was part of the original manor. Adjacent to the church is the Sleepy Hollow Cemetery, formerly the Tarrytown Cemetery until Washington Irving petitioned to rename it to 'keep that beautiful and umbrageous neighborhood sacred from the anti-poetical and all-leveling axe' and 'to secure the patronage of all desirous of sleeping quietly in their graves.'

In fact, Washington Irving is buried here in a section called Beekman Mound; other section names include Poet's Mound and Sunnyside. The whole place has a mysterious air about it, especially on a foggy morning, when the curvy lanes make getting lost seem like a prelude to a horror movie. Stop in at the office for a map of the cemetery.

KYKUIT
☎ 914-631-9491; 2hr tour adult/senior/student $20/19/17; ⏰10am-2:45pm Mon & Wed-Sun Apr-Nov

Perhaps no family has had a larger influence on 20th-century American history than the Rockefellers, who have left their stamp on business, domestic politics and international relations. The family fortune was founded by John D Rockefeller (1839–1937), an Ohio-born entrepreneur who bought into an oil refinery in 1859. In the years following the end of the Civil War, his Standard Oil Company evolved into a formidable monopoly with a hammerlock on crude oil processing and sales in the US. By the time the company was broken into 34 different companies by the US Supreme Court in 1911, John D Rockefeller had amassed a fortune worth more than $1 billion. (Standard Oil's constituent parts are now huge businesses in their own rights and include Exxon, Mobil, Texaco, Amoco, British Petroleum, Shell, Chevron and Atlantic Richfield.)

A small portion of Rockefeller's fortune went to build this Neoclassical mansion, on a high bluff overlooking the Hudson. It was home to several generations of Rockefellers, and parts of the estate are still used by family members. Essentially a fine-art gallery, it is almost impossible to imagine that people conducted day-to-day rituals inside a building more akin to a bank or a branch of government. Tong Dynasty porcelain and famous paintings (including a Gilbert Stuart portrait of George Washington) adorn the interior. Outside, the exquisite garden overlooking the Hudson River ('Kykuit,' pronounced 'K-eye-CUT,' is the Dutch word for 'lookout') is home to modern sculptures by Henry Moore, Alexander Calder, Jacques Lipchitz, Alberto Giacometti, Pablo Picasso and others.

The basement gallery is the most intimate space of Kykuit. This is where Nelson Rockefeller (1908–79), the patriarch's grandson, enjoyed his collection of modern artwork. Nelson served Presidents Roosevelt, Truman and Eisenhower in a variety of positions and helped establish the current site of the Museum of Modern Art in New York City. He was also elected governor of New York State for four terms. Nelson was a socially liberal Republican who was so self-conscious of his wealth that he used the phrase 'thanks a thousand' to express gratitude. A leading contender for the Republican presidential nomination in the 1960, 1964 and 1968 elections, Nelson was appointed by President Gerald Ford to serve as vice

Flower Power

In the spring and fall, the best features of many of the historic homes along the Hudson River are their gardens, which were often designed with as much care and expense as the homes. Gardens are open from dawn to dusk, and admission is typically free (unless otherwise noted). Lilacs, roses and fall color are major draws at the following standouts:

- **Montgomery Place** (p30) **& Clermont State Historic Site** (p31) – With tree-framed views of the Hudson River and the Catskill Mountains, these nearby estates tie for the honor of most beautiful grounds.
- **Vanderbilt Mansion** (p23) – The formal Italian rose garden is straight out of the plans for a European palace.
- **Innisfree Garden** (p36) – Devoted to landscape art, this garden incorporates the wild and the sculpted into a seamless balance.
- **Lyndhurst** (p10) – Put your sniffer to the rose-smelling test when this exceptional rose garden springs into action.

president following Richard Nixon's resignation in 1974. Even today, left-leaning members of the GOP are known derisively as 'Rockefeller Republicans.'

Reservations are essential to visit Kykuit; on weekends, chances are slim that you will join a tour if you simply show up in a hopeful mood. If you do decide to trust your luck, go in the morning, get on the day's wait list and wait around on the deck in back, or stroll across the bridge to the mill to get away from the mob scene in the gift shop. Children are discouraged from attending tours of Kykuit – something about noise and vast wealth being incompatible. All tours leave by shuttle bus from outside the Philipsburg Manor. The basic tour lasts about two hours and includes the house, galleries and garden. More involved tours ($35, 3 hrs) take in the sculpture garden, the 3rd floor of the house and other add-ons.

UNION CHURCH AT POCANTICO HILLS
☎ 914-332-6659; River Rd, Pocantico; $4; ⌚11am-5pm Mon & Wed-Fri, 10am-5pm Sat, 2-5pm Sun Apr-Dec

This old, stone church must be seen from the inside out. It's home to several stained-glass windows by Henri Matisse and Marc Chagall; the modern-art treasures were commissioned by the Rockefeller family and were completed between 1954 and 1965. Most of Chagall's nine windows are dedicated to Old Testament prophets. Matisse's beautiful rose window was his last completed work of art. The church is best visited on a sunny day to see the stained glass in its full glory. Call beforehand if visiting on a Saturday, as sometimes the church hosts weddings.

To reach the church, go north from Tarrytown about 2 miles, and turn right (east) just before Philipsburg Manor onto Route 448. The church is about 3 miles down on your right.

VAN CORTLANDT MANOR
☎ 914-271-8981, 914-631-8200 reservations; S Riverside Ave, Croton-on-Hudson; adult/senior/child $9/8/5, grounds pass $4; ⌚10am-5pm Mon & Wed-Fri Apr-Oct

This living history museum introduces visitors to the Van Cortlandts, a Dutch family influential during the 'new nation' period (1790–1815). The home and 200-year-old gardens overlook both the Hudson and the Croton rivers. The furnishings are a major attraction; perhaps three quarters of the family's original possessions are on display, from Queen Anne and Chippendale furniture to the contents of the colonial kitchen, including pots and pans, jugs, mixing bowls and graters. There's not a microwave in sight. There is even a milk room with a stone floor for cold storage. For a telling sign of the social politics of the day, notice the gun-slits built into the sides of several outer walls, a reminder of the failure to live peacefully with the native inhabitants of the area.

An annual microbrewery fair is held here in honor of the patriarch Olaf Van Cortlandt, who made his fortune as a brewmeister in New Amsterdam. If you're interested in focusing on a particular historical aspect (decorative arts, herbal medicines and African American history connected to the site), call the office about the availability of such tours.

ROCKEFELLER STATE PARK PRESERVE

☎ 914-631-1470; Rte 117; parking $6; open year-round

Three miles north of Sleepy Hollow is the entrance to this peaceful and beautiful getaway from the hustle and bustle of historic touring. The preserve is a rolling, woodsy expanse of solitude, with old fields and pastures marked by low stone walls. A free walking tour map is available at the small administrative building, and a large notice board tells some of the area's history, from the times of the earliest Munsee-speaking Indian people to the developers of the New Netherlands to the Rockefeller benefactors.

A short trail from the entrance will put you on the edge of small Swan Lake. The preserve's entrance is just 1 mile east of Route 9, about a mile north of Philipsburg Manor.

SLEEPING

Accommodations in Tarrytown are corporate facilities geared toward the business traveler. Weekday rates tend to be higher than weekends, and if a conference is in town it is difficult to get a room on short notice. If you get stuck without a crash pad, head up to **Peekskill** (p16).

Courtyard by Marriott (☎ 914-631-1122; 475 White Plains Rd/Hwy 119; d $165-200), **Hampton Inn** (☎ 914-592-5680; 200 Tarrytown Rd, Elmsford; d $125-150) and **Tarrytown Hilton Inn** (☎ 914-631-5700; 455 S Broadway/Hwy 9; d $160-200) comprise the meager options.

EATING & ENTERTAINMENT

BELLA'S RESTAURANT & DONUT SHOP
☎ 914-332-0444; 5 S Broadway cnr Main St; mains $5-10; ⏰5am-9pm Mon-Sat, 7am-3pm Sun

One of the best diners in the valley, Bella's bakes donuts that will tempt even those who swore off donuts years ago. Bella's also serves goulash, pot roast, hearty soups and sandwiches, and you might just detect an Irish lilt in your server's accent.

LEFTERI'S GYRO RESTAURANT
☎ 914-524-9687; 1 N Main St cnr Broadway; mains $10-12; ⏰11am-10pm Mon-Sun

For homemade Greek food, try this small, family-run business. It serves big pita sandwiches (chicken, beef or veggie) and homemade Greek pastries; the 'small' Greek salad is a meal in itself. The restaurant is on a busy corner with outside seating and lots of people-watching. And despite the restaurant's crowds, the waitstaff knows how to move the food to the people.

MAIN STREET CAFÉ
☎ 914-332-9834; 24 Main St; mains $10-20; ⏰12-3pm & 5-10pm Tue-Sat, 12-9pm Sun

An upscale American bistro, Main Street Café has standard sandwiches (portobello mushroom or London broil) and half orders of seafood pasta. In the summer, there are outside tables on the Main St sidewalk.

TARRYTOWN MUSIC HALL
☎ 914-631-3390; 13 Main St

If you start feeling depressed from visiting too many mansions, you can return to 'architectural Earth' with a quick visit to this performing arts center. Housed in an 1885 Queen Anne building and listed in the National Register of Historic Places, the music hall presents jazz, classical and folk concerts as well as dance, opera, musicals, dramas and children's theater.

ON THE ROAD: ROUTE 9

North of Sleepy Hollow, **Ossining** is a handsome riverside village of barbershops and hardware stores. If the name of the town sounds strangely familiar, you're on to something. The town used to be called Sing Sing, until the 1820s prison eclipsed the town's good name. Before the death penalty was abolished in New York State in 1965, Sing Sing was the primary facility for capital punishment by means of electrocution. (New York reinstated the death penalty in 1995, but no executions have taken place in the state since 1963). This and other facts about being sent 'up the river' are available at the small **Ossining Visitor Center & Museum** (☎914-941-0009; 95 Broadway; admission free; ⏰10am-4pm Mon-Sat), inside the community center. An old electric chair and lifesize replicas of prison cells are also on display. The **Ossining Historical Museum** (☎914-941-0001; 196 Croton Ave; admission free; ⊙hours vary) houses Indian artifacts, antique dolls and items from nearby Sing Sing Prison.

PEEKSKILL

Population 22,400; Map 3

Peekskill is a homely town with a big, adorable heart. The active arts scene, reasonable accommodations and a great bookstore make up for what the town might lack in the faux-antique department.

SIGHTS & ACTIVITIES

BRUISED APPLE
☎914-734-7000; 923 Central Ave; ⊙10am-6pm Mon-Fri, 12-6pm Sun

Manhattan bibliophiles make the trek out here to visit this used bookstore featuring floor-to-high-ceiling stacks of used, rare and out-of-print books. There are good sections on local history, art, travel and exploration. A groovy selection of used LPs and CDs competes for collectors' attention.

UNDERGROUND RAILROAD SITES
☎917-736-7908 tour information; waymondbrothers@yahoo.com; suggested donation $10

Peekskill was one of many 'stations' for slaves escaping to the emancipated north. Historians believe that 75,000 slaves gained their freedom via Peekskill and that many were led through the state by one of the country's most heralded railroad conductors, Harriet Tubman. To visit the safe houses and hear the stories of such a journey, join the Underground Railroad Tours, conducted four times a year by local historian Waymond Brothers. For groups of 10 or more, Waymond can also arrange additional tours with advance reservation. Within the next two years the proposed Museum of the Underground Railroad should be open to the public. Stop into the **Fern Tree** (☎914-737-3600; 13 S Division St), an African gift shop, to inquire on the progress of the museum or to obtain additional information about Peekskill's role in the Underground Railroad.

OPEN STUDIOS
☎914-739-2333; 1008 Brown St; guided tours adults/seniors $10/8; 3rd Sat of every month

To peek into the artistic creations of Peekskill, plan a trip during open studios. Call the Paramount Center for the Arts (p17) for details. For more insight into the art scene here, join the guided two-hour tour held during open studios; tours meet at the Paramount Center for the Arts at 10:45am (call to confirm).

PARAMOUNT CENTER FOR THE ARTS
☎ 914-739-2333; 1009 Brown St; ☷10am-6pm Mon-Fri, noon-4pm Sat

This restored movie house shows excellent international and independent films, which generally change every two days. The theater is also the setting for occasional concerts and plays.

SLEEPING & EATING

PEEKSKILL INN
☎ 914-739-1500, 800-526-9466; 634 Main St; d $117-130; pet-friendly; ☒ ☐

Near the junction of Routes 9 and 6, this motel-inn is perched high on a bluff overlooking the river and a few 'castles on the Rhine' (industrial factories). The staff's enthusiasm for Peekskill is infectious, and you might find yourself more charmed than you had expected. Appalachian Trail hikers stop in frequently for creature comforts before resuming their journeys.

More River, Less Asphalt

If driving the river road sounds too much like work, climb aboard a river cruise or paddle a kayak for some tête-à-tête with the Hudson.

New York Waterway (☎ 800-533-3779; www.nywaterway.com) offers the following package tours to historic sites. Most cruise boats depart from Pier 78 at W 38th St and Twelfth Ave in Manhattan.

- **Sleepy Hollow Cruise** (adult/senior/child $46/44/25) takes in Washington Irving's Sunnyside home and Philipsburg Manor. The ticket price includes boat fare, ground transportation and admission.
- **Kykuit Cruise** (adult/senior $64/59) includes site admission, and the trip lasts a total of 7-1/2 hours. Small children are really discouraged from visiting Kykuit.
- **North Hudson Cruise** (adult/child $15/8) departs Tarrytown (at the foot of Main St) for a two-hour trip up the Hudson to Peekskill Mountains.

Hudson River Recreation (☎ 888-321-4837; www.kayakhudson.com) leads guided paddle tours from Sleepy Hollow, Nyack and New Rochelle, exploring the river's history and inlets.

Hudson River Kayak Tours (☎ 845-876-0246; www.nykayaks.com; $55; reservations recommended) leads guided tours from Rhinebeck through the Rondout Creek, where skeleton barges have banked. Another tour recommended for beginners is through the graceful Tivoli Bay, magnanimously watched over by **Montgomery Place** (p30).

Hudson River Valley Ramble (☎ 800-453-6665; www.hudsonvalleyramble.com) occurs on two weekends in September with a variety of outdoor hikes or kayak trips led by trained naturalists, ecologists, geologists and historians.

CHOLA CUENCANA RESTAURANT

☎ 914-737-9041; 1101 Main St; lunch buffet $6; ✹9am-8pm Mon-Fri

While traveling through the Hudson Valley, it is easy to get bistro-overloaded. Thankfully, this Ecuadorian restaurant saves people from eating too many mesclun salads. Dust off your Spanish skills and head here for an enormous, down-home lunch buffet (weekdays only).

PEEKSKILL COFFEE HOUSE

☎ 914-739-1287; 101 S Division St; ✹6am-9pm Sun-Thu, 6am-11pm Fri & Sat

This cozy coffee shop serves steamy cups of joe as well as Friday night music and poetry readings (no cover, 8pm).

SUSAN'S

☎ 914-737-6624; 12 N Division St; mains $10-15; ✹12-2:30pm & 5:30-9pm Tue-Sat

Right downtown, Susan's is where most of the town's business is informally decided. The American bistro-style dishes include salmon-strudel with spinach and wild rice, and Louisiana shrimp and andouille sausage jambalaya.

ON THE ROAD: ROUTE 9 TO ROUTE 403

North of Peekskill, Route 9 crawls into some beautiful scenery with glimpses of rocky highlands across the river and lush groves of woods exultant and reverential. Follow the Route 403 split toward the town of Garrison and on to **Boscobel** (☎ 845-265-3638; www.boscobel.org; 1601 Route 9D, Garrison; adult/senior/child $10/9/7; ✹9:30am-4:15pm Wed-Mon). Boscobel

Biking in the Hudson Valley

From tricky root-studded trails to quiet country roads, Hudson Valley offers diverse mountain- and road-bike riding opportunities. By far the greatest mountain biking is around New Paltz. **Minnewaska State Park** (p46) has a series of popular carriage trails, as does nearby **Mohonk Preserve** (p47) and the **Wallkill Valley Rail Trail** (p46). On the opposite side of the river, **Mills-Norrie State Park** (p25) and **Clarence Fahnestock State Park** (p35) also have scenic but challenging trails.

By touring the country roads around Hudson, Rhinebeck and West Point, you can combine a strenuous ride with visits to nearby attractions. Bike shops in the area can provide route details and suggestions.

Before tearing down the trail, find out about appropriate permits and helmet rules, and be aware that most trails are multiuse.

is one of the best examples of Federal-style architecture and decorative arts, with a magnificent view of the Hudson River posing at the foot of a sweeping lawn. Built in 1804, it was the home of States Morris Dyckman (1755–1806), an accountant and loyalist hailing from tavern-keeping parents. He rose to great esteem and then fell just as quickly due to some dodgy bookkeeping (predating Enron's numbers' tampering). After changing hands for several generations, the house was sold at auction in the 1950s for $35 to a demolition contractor. That is when Lila Acheson Wallace, cofounder of the *Reader's Digest*, financially backed the house's restoration and acquisition of a remarkable collection by legendary cabinetmaker Duncan Phyfe. (Phyfe's grand Federal-style decorative pieces drip with ornamentation and echo the design images used in classical furniture.)

COLD SPRING

Population 1900; Map 1

Cold Spring is a romantic town with prim townhouses lining the narrow streets and a quiet river promenade in the shadow of Storm King Mountain. Midway between Peekskill and Beacon, Cold Spring (on Route 9D) serves as a scenic base for touring sights in either of these cities. Many people make weekend antiquing trips to Cold Spring – often arriving via the train from New York City – and the shops and restaurants are reflective of this affluent clientele. A walking tour sponsored by the **Putnam County Historical Society** (☎ 845-265-4010; 63 Chestnut St) begins at 72 Main St. The tour is offered on Sunday at 2pm from mid-May to mid-November. Call for additional information, or inquire at any of the antique shops on Main St.

Pig Hill Inn (☎ 845-265-9247; 73 Main St; d $120-170 weekday, $150-220 weekend, includes breakfast) is a brick Victorian in the middle of the village and has antique-decorated rooms with shared and private baths. The Tranquility Room comes with a fireplace.

East Side Kitchen (☎ 845-265-7723; 124 Main St; mains $10-15; 12-9pm Tue-Sun) is a revival country general store of retro-chic mint greens. This stylish spot has magnificent salads and a loyal clientele of precocious children. How old were you when you were introduced to calamari? These kids have you beat.

The Depot (☎ 845-265-5000; www.coldspringdepot.com; 1 Depot Rd; mains $10-18; 11am-10pm Mon-Thu, 11am-11pm Fri, 1-11pm Sat, 1-10pm Sun) is right by the train tracks, as you'll soon discover, and is actually a converted train lounge. In the summer, several umbrella-shaded outdoor tables vibrate slightly as the train goes by. Inside, a lovely horseshoe bar also affords a quick glimpse of the passing trains. Food options range from fish and chicken to burgers and pasta.

ON THE ROAD: ROUTE 9D TO ROUTE 9

Leaving Cold Spring, you climb north out of the valley into the struggling burg of **Beacon**. Once a proud factory town, it sunk into a long economic descent after the factories fled south and west. Today, the handsome business district is slowly being gussied up by galleries and gourmet eateries, but there is still a very prominent contingent of winos, public urinators and shifty gas station loiterers. A recent boon to Beacon was delivered by the Manhattan-based museum, Dia, which has staked out a satellite exhibition space in a refurbished Nabisco box factory. Now the art world leaves New York City (gasp!) for a town once synonymous with 'cesspool.'

Dia: Beacon (☎ 845-440-0100; 3 Beekman St; adult/student $10/ 7; 🕙11am-6pm Thu-Mon Apr-Oct, 11am-4pm Fri-Mon Nov-Mar) comprises 240,000 square feet of exhibition space that is impressive in its own right. Light streams through the skylights, illuminating the enormous raw space of stark, white walls and torturous echoes of squeaking shoes. Before engaging the exhibits, first put yourself in a 'modern art' state of mind. That's right: modern art doesn't have to be beautiful or realistic or intricate. In order to achieve its goal, modern art has to affect you either by eliciting disgust or wonder. This it will do. Works by John Chamberlain, Andy Warhol, Blinky Palermo and others alter space, distort perception or prove your suspicion that artists are certifiably insane.

To get to the museum, follow Route 9D through town and make a left at city hall. Go past the I-84 intersection and turn right on to the street in front of the Season's Restaurant; this is Beekman St, and the museum is down the road on your left.

Route 9 loses much of its pastoral appeal as it leaves Beacon and travels through Poughkeepsie and Hyde Park, where it swells to a six-lane highway lined with strip malls. If you're back-roading to points farther north than Hyde Park, consider backtracking to Peekskill and jumping on the Bear Mountain Parkway, which will connect you to the picturesque **Taconic State Parkway** (p35).

Poughkeepsie ('pooh-KIP-see') is the largest town on the east bank of the Hudson and has suffered the same urban fate as its southern neighbor Beacon; as industry moved out, decay moved

Lincoln's Appetite

During the Civil War, President Abraham Lincoln visited Cold Spring to inspect the cannons that had been made in the village. To demonstrate their power, locals fired the cannons at the facing cliffs across the river. According to the *WPA Guide to New York* (1940), Lincoln remarked, 'I'm confident you can hit that mountain over there, so suppose we get something to eat. I'm hungry.

in. However, there are a few historic sites worth a detour. **Vassar College** (☎845-437-7000; 124 College Ave cnr Raymond Ave), a well-respected liberal arts school, offers tours of its 125-acre campus daily during the summer months. Vassar is also home to the **Francis Lehman Loeb Art Center** (☎845-437-5632; admission free; ۞10am-5pm Tue-Sat, 1-5pm Sun), which contains several paintings from the Hudson River school.

Samuel FB Morse Historic Site (Locust Grove; ☎845-454-4500; 370 South Rd/Route 9; house adult/senior/student $7/6/3, grounds free; ۞house 10am-3pm May-Nov, grounds 8am-dusk), a privately-owned 1830 mansion about 2 miles south of the Mid-Hudson Bridge, is the former home of telegraph inventor and artist Samuel FB Morse. The house, built in the Tuscan villa style popular in the mid-19th century, has picture windows designed to showcase the 150-acre manicured grounds, whose carriage roads wind through locust, hemlock and larch trees and gardens galore. It's also home to a beautiful wildlife and bird sanctuary with easy hiking trails as well as a visitors center, a gallery and a museum shop. In addition to the ornate mansion furnishings, some of Morse's old telegraph equipment and paintings are displayed. Check out the mirror in the butler's pantry and the kitchen – it's carefully positioned for the staff to follow progress at the dining table without disturbing the family or guests.

Although Morse is remembered as one of the great inventors, his true passion was painting. He seems to have invented things in order to support his painting habit. For an eight-year period, he was in and out of court over patent rights, but he continued painting the entire time.

HYDE PARK

Population 20,800; Map 4

Hyde Park is forever associated with the Roosevelts and their homes, with separate historic sites for Franklin Delano Roosevelt and his wife Eleanor. In marked contrast is the ostentatious summer cottage of the Vanderbilts.

Sadly, the surviving town of Hyde Park has developed little of its own allure. In a region of preserved hamlets, Hyde Park instead developed a serious strip-mall addiction concentrated on Route 9, right alongside the town's historic homes. If there is a walkable downtown, it does a good job of hiding. Although you'll be more married to your car here than other stops along the route, Hyde Park is the most convenient and affordable base for the Roosevelt sites.

SIGHTS & ACTIVITIES

HOME OF FRANKLIN D ROOSEVELT NATIONAL HISTORIC SITE

FDR Site: ☎845-229-9115, 800-967-2283 reservations; 519 Albany Post Rd/Rte 9; adult/child $14/free; ۞9am-5pm

Top Cottage: ☎ 845-229-9115, 800-967-2283 reservations; adult/child $8/free; ⊙10am, 1pm & 3pm Thu-Mon May-Oct

One of the most popular presidents of modern America, Franklin Delano Roosevelt (FDR) was born to an influential New York family, the lineage of which can be traced to Dutch fur traders and included founders of the Bank of New York, a US president (Teddy Roosevelt) and railroad tycoons. Despite privilege and pedigree, FDR developed a keen sense of social responsibility, which manifested itself most notably during his presidency in the work and relief programs he initiated to help offset the economic disaster of the 1930s. At the age of 39, just as he was poised to make a bid for the White House, he contracted polio and never regained the use of his legs. This was for FDR but a temporary setback; he resumed the political stump three years later and was elected president four consecutive times, governing the country through the Great Depression and most of WWII. Not bad for a man confined to a wheelchair and who never finished his law degree at Columbia University.

Even in the staid environment of a historical monument, FDR's compelling and charming persona emerges. This historic site includes FDR's home, library-museum, gravesite and rose garden. Guided tours of FDR's home, Springwood, take visitors through a surprisingly ordinary home of practical tastes. In the bedroom that looks like a 1950s TV show, Winston Churchill spent the night. The home was outfitted with a hand-pulled elevator to transport FDR and his chair to the 2nd floor. Because the tour guides allow visitors to wander around on their own, children have the opportunity to indulge their curiosity throughout the site. Tours are popular, and reservations are encouraged.

The Museum of the Franklin D Roosevelt Library is the nation's first presidential library and the only one that was ever put to use by a sitting president. Several exhibits at the museum highlight the WPA and other relief programs, along with exhibits about Pearl Harbor and America's entry into WWII. The museum features old photos, FDR's

Sailing for the Hudson

Activist and folk singer Pete Seeger joined with a group of friends in 1966 to 'build a boat to save a river.' Their brainstorming resulted in a replica of a Dutch sailing sloop, called *Clearwater*, that would educate people about river health, conservation and pollution. At this time the Hudson was a dumping ground for raw sewage and industrial waste. The *Clearwater* helped ignite conservation attempts on the river and even sailed to Washington, DC, to lobby for passage of the Clean Water Act. Today the sloop and the affiliated environmental group monitor activities on the river and introduce visitors to educational exhibits. Visit the *Clearwater* organization's website (www.clearwater.org) for a schedule of sailings and volunteer opportunities.

voice on tape (from his 'fireside chats' and several speeches), and a special wing in memory of Eleanor Roosevelt. Also on display is FDR's famous 1936 Ford Phaeton car – equipped with special hand controls so he could drive despite the restricted mobility caused by his bout with polio. Roosevelt's White House desk is also here, supposedly just as he left it on his last day at work in 1945, less than a year after he was elected to a record fourth term as president.

A new site open to visitors is **Top Cottage**, FDR's private retreat. British monarchs and other world figures attended informal diplomacy meetings here; one widely reported event was when King George VI and Queen Elizabeth were served hot dogs at a Top Cottage picnic. Tickets for the site are available from the booth at the FDR National Historic Site.

ELEANOR ROOSEVELT NATIONAL HISTORIC SITE
☎ 845-229-9115, 800-967-2283 reservations; adult/child $8/free; ✆9am-5pm daily May-Oct, 10am-4pm Sat & Sun Apr, Nov & Dec

Better known as Val-Kill, Dutch for 'Valley Stream,' this site is 2 miles east of Hyde Park. Eleanor herself used to make the drive frequently, and townspeople apparently pulled over to the curb quickly when she came by – not so much out of their respect and admiration for the popular First Lady, but rather due to their knowledge of her erratic driving habits.

Eleanor Roosevelt used Val-Kill as a retreat from the main house at Hyde Park, in part to pursue her own interests and maintain her own identity. The cottage, as she called it, was her own place – not FDR's and not his mother's. After the president's death, Eleanor made this her permanent home.

Although she was raised in society, Eleanor's house is a simple cottage in the true sense of the word. Unlike many of the famous residences up and down the Hudson, Val-Kill was not meant to impress anyone; comfort was a priority, and you see it immediately in the ordinary and nonmatching furniture, the everyday chinaware and the plain restaurant water glasses. This was the dinnerware she used to entertain statesmen, kings and queens, and the local students she invited for dinner. The grounds are dotted with sugar maple and pine trees, and a road leads to the cottage from the entrance off Route 9G.

Eleanor was involved in human rights before the term was coined, and she helped establish the International Declaration of Human Rights, earning her the designation 'first lady of the world.' Instead of great works of art, the wood-paneled walls of the cottage are crammed with family photos.

VANDERBILT MANSION NATIONAL HISTORIC SITE
☎ 845-229-9115, 800-967-2283; Albany Post Rd/Rte 9; adult/child $8/free; ✆9am-5pm

Another valley spectacle, this mansion housed Frederick, grandson of Cornelius 'Commodore' Vanderbilt, and his wife, Louise. Commodore made his money the new-fangled way: he earned it ruthlessly. He started out as a farmer in Staten Island, created a ferry company at the age of 16, and soon bought up all the struggling railroads to amass

Docent Lingo

Architectural styles go by so many aliases that it is nearly impossible to sort out all the mumbo-jumbo that guidebooks and tour leaders throw at you during a house tour. This quick and dirty primer might help you sort out the most popular styles found in the Hudson Valley, but you're on your own with spotting a transom from a lintel.

Federal – The most ubiquitous of early styles, Federal (1780–1820) defined a uniquely American expression, drawing from the republics of the ancient world. Homes were designed with very plain but regal facades and exhibited a devotion to symmetry (a central hallway balanced by an equal number of rooms on each side). The entry door was usually adorned with a fanlight (window shaped like an open fan). Federal homes were favored in compact downtowns; Thomas Cole's house in **Catskill** (p58) and Martin Van Buren's home **Lindenwald** (p34) are both examples.

Greek Revival – The new republic looked once again to the classical world for design inspiration in the 1800s. What emerged was an appreciation of Greek temple architecture, including facades of columns perched on a pediment. Government buildings are the main examples of Greek Revival, while private homes incorporated certain design elements. **Staatsburgh** (p25) is an example of Greek Revival.

Beaux Arts – Also known as Neoclassical or Classical Revival, this style flourished from the late 1800s to early 1900s and looked to – you guessed it – Greece and Rome for inspiration. Beaux Arts differs from its predecessors in its elaborate ornamentation, including colonnaded windows or projecting pavilions. Architects trained at Paris' École des Beaux-Arts were the biggest proponents of the style, which was typically so grandiose that only government institutions could carry it well. William Wells Bosworth was one of the country's main Beaux Arts architects; he designed the MIT campus in Cambridge, Massachusetts, and the Rockefeller house, **Kykuit** (p11), in Tarrytown, New York.

Gothic Revival – This style (1830s to '40s) was the architectural arm of a larger literary and philosophical movement known as the Aesthetic or Romantic period. Rebelling against the emergence of the machine age, Romantics looked to the 'innocent' period of the European medieval times for inspiration. This resulted in a revival of elements used in medieval churches, such as steeply pitched roofs and gables. In the Hudson Valley in particular, the Aesthetic movement was extended to landscape design. Andrew Jackson Downing and his associate Calvert Vaux used the contours of the land for a complementary effect. Rather than a military formation of ponds, roses and walkways used in traditional formal gardens, Downing and Vaux created winding lanes and undulating lawns that would frame scenic vistas of the river. Nearly every historic home in the Hudson Valley exemplifies some influence of Gothic Revival.

a transportation empire. Despite his power and wealth, Commodore was ostracized from New York society for being a commoner. His descendants, however, rose up the social ladder, partly due to their excessive display of wealth. This Beaux Arts monument – an eclectic mix of classical Greek, Roman and Baroque lines – was merely a country palace used on weekends or seasonal getaways, but was painstakingly decorated to emulate the styles of European aristocracy. Within a generation, the house was so flamboyant that the heirs couldn't find a buyer and ultimately donated it to the public trust. The Vanderbilt Mansion is about 2 miles north of Hyde Park on Route 9.

STAATSBURGH STATE HISTORIC SITE
☎ 845-889-8851; Albany Post Rd (Route 9), Staatsburg; adult/student/senior/child $5/4/4/1; ⏱10am-5pm Sat, 12-5pm Sun Apr-Oct

About 5 miles north of Hyde Park, this historic site (formerly known as Mills Mansion) is an updated Greek Revival-style building with requisite white columns in front and designed by the famous New York City firm of McKim, Mead & White. It was built in 1832 and remodeled in 1896. This was no ordinary addition – it's ostentatious to the extreme. The house is said to have served as the example of the Trenors' retreat, Bellomont, in Edith Wharton's novel *The House of Mirth*. There are guided house tours every half hour (otherwise, you'd get lost amid the 65 rooms). The palatial grounds at the site are open year-round.

SLEEPING & EATING

MILLS-NORRIE STATE PARK
☎ 800-456-2267; www.reserveamerica.com; Rte 9, Staatsburg; tent $14

About 2 miles from Staatsburgh State Historic Park, this 1000-acre park has camping, a marina, boat launch, bicycle paths, sledding, cross-country skiing, nature trails and a museum. The rough terrain of the Norrie Point-Ogden Mills trail is a favorite of experienced mountain bikers. You'll also find Norrie Point Environmental Site, which has a small aquarium that replicates conditions of the Hudson River. Cabins (night/week $62.50/250) look out over the river. This is also a convenient spot between Hyde Park and tony Rhinebeck for the back-to-nature set.

COSTELLO'S GUEST HOUSE
☎ 845-229-2559; 21 Main St; d $55-65

Patsy Costello rents out two rooms in her home; both rooms share a bath. She also offers discounts for weekly stays, especially if you're in town to do research on FDR. The house is two blocks from the Vanderbilt mansion.

ROOSEVELT INN
☎ 845-229-2443, fax 845-229-0026; 4360 Albany Post Rd/Rte 9; d from $65, suite $95-135, includes breakfast; 🖭

This family-friendly roadside motel is halfway between the FDR and Vanderbilt sites. Rooms in the back are less noisy than those facing the road.

CULINARY INSTITUTE OF AMERICA

CIA; ☎ 845-471-6608 reservations; www.ciachef.edu; 1946 Campus Dr

This is the preeminent culinary school in the US. To sample the creations of America's next generation of chefs, you need reservations at one of the four restaurants on the campus: Ristorante Caterina de' Medici (Italian), Escoffier Restaurant (French), American Bounty (American Regional) and St Andrew's Café (the least formal and least expensive). Business-casual attire is recommended and reservations should be made Monday through Friday.

Lunch is served from 11:30am to 1pm sharp, and dinner is served from 6:30 to 8:30 pm sharp. Escoffier and American Bounty are open Tuesday through Saturday; Caterina and St Andrew's Café are open Monday through Friday. In the restaurants, lunch mains start at $15 to $25, and dinner mains start at $20 to $35; St Andrew's starts at $10 to $15. Another addition to CIA's spread is the informal Apple Pie Bakery Café, a student-staffed eatery open Monday to Friday.

EVEREADY DINER

☎ 845-229-8100; 540 Albany Post Rd/Rte 9; mains $7-10

Between Poughkeepsie and Hyde Park, this busy art-deco diner has a bit of everything, like Brooklyn egg creams and pastrami sandwiches. But who could pass up their disco fries, the John Travolta of gravy fries complete with bacon? Your heart never had it so good.

RHINEBECK

Population 3000; Map 6

With proud Victorian homes and well-pressed residents, Rhinebeck is so pretty and romantic that it feels like a movie set, lacking the messiness of ordinary life. Before it became a weekend getaway for well-heeled New Yorkers, the town was a stagecoach stop and still boasts the famous Beekman Arms, America's oldest continuously operating inn. Rates have changed over the years, but a sign in the lobby recalls another era:

Lodging 3 pence
With breakfast, 4 pence
Only 5 lodgers to a bed
No boots can be worn in bed.

Although there are many historic homes to visit north of Rhinebeck, the most popular activity is to spend the day sleeping late, brunching at a fashionable restaurant and strolling the small downtown. If you're a real go-getter, you can even use Rhinebeck as a base for visiting Hyde Park and Millbrook, but that is ambitious.

The only example of a Queen Anne (Victorian) house museum on the river, **Wilderstein** (☎ 845-876-4818; Morton Rd, Rhinebeck; adult/student/child $8/5/free; ☽12-3:30pm Thu-Sun May-Oct) is a must for any shabby chicster. The house was inherited directly from the establishing family's last occupant (Margaret Suckley) and boasts 44 stained-glass windows designed by Tiffany & Co. But before your imagination flies to *Architectural Digest* spreads, here's a little background: Miss Suckley was a spinster of a declining family fortune and, in the taped interview of her taking tea on the front porch, she describes how the house has aged right along with her. While the house has outlived her, its longevity is quite evident in the exterior chipped paint and the molding damask wallpaper. The parts of the house that have yet to be restored give a realistic perspective on the monumental task of historic preservation and a glimpse at the sunset years of a once financially prominent family. In May, stop by for the Fala-lookalike contest, honoring the Scotch terrier (named

Farmers for a Day

The Hudson Valley has long been a rich agricultural area. Old-timers swear by the sweet corn, but signaling out one crop would be unfair to the bounty, from strawberries and tomatoes to apples and pears. There are hundreds of local farms, produce stands and 'pick-your-own' farms in the region. Mid- to late summer is the best time to visit, of course, but check on the harvest schedule; depending on the weather, rain and so forth, harvest times vary.

The pick-your-own system works like this: you are given a container (tray or basket), you pick what you want from the seasonal fruits and vegetables, you weigh your pickings at the register and you pay wholesale prices.

Of the many regional farms, the following offer a decent cross-section of agricultural outings.

Greig Farm (☎ 845-758-1234; ⏰9am-5pm Apr-Dec, extended summer hours) occupies the whole of Pitcher Lane, 3 miles north of Red Hook, between Routes 9 and 9G. It's a one-stop produce market with a bakery and education center. Popular produce pickings in the mid- to late summer include asparagus, peas, strawberries, blueberries, blackberries, raspberries, a dozen varieties of apples (Empire, Jonathan, Rome, etc) and pumpkins – especially popular before Halloween. There is also a cut-your-own flower garden, as well as a picnic area and a weekend snack bar.

Keepsake Farms (☎ 845-897-2266; E Hook Cross Rd; ⏰9am-6pm May-Sept, 9am-5pm Oct-Apr) is a very good produce market and pick-your-own farm, just south of I-84 and a mile west of the Taconic State Parkway (the nearest town is Fishkill). Apples, pumpkin, berries and more are available, but if you are after a certain fruit or vegetable, call ahead to be sure it's harvest time.

LoveApple Farm (☎ 518-828-5048; www.loveapplefarm.com; 1421 Route 9H, Ghent) is down the road from the Martin Van Buren home, Lindenwald, outside of **Kinderhook** (p34). There is a petting zoo, a farmers market, fresh-baked pies and pick-your-own apples.

Fala) that Miss Suckley gave to the Roosevelts. Fala had the honor of being the official White House dog during FDR's tenure.

If the Red Baron is a personal hero or you have kids in tow, you should visit the **Old Rhinebeck Aerodrome** (☎ 845-758-8610; Stone Church Rd; museum adult/senior/child $6/5/2, air show $12/10/5; ⏱museum 10am-5pm mid-May–Oct; air shows 2pm Sat & Sun mid-Jun–mid-Oct). Between Rhinebeck and Red Hook, this combination museum and air show has vintage planes from WWI and antique cars; you can even take a ride in an open cockpit plane, but you have to provide your own scarf and goggles.

SLEEPING

THE VILLAGE INN OF RHINEBECK
☎ 845-876-7000, fax 845-876-4756; 6260 Rte 9; d weekday/weekend $70/90
This roadside motel has large rooms with windows that look out over a suburban yard. The owner has an interesting collection of baseball memorabilia displayed in the lobby.

BEEKMAN ARMS
☎ 845-876-7077; 6387 Mill St/Rte 9; d $110-180; pet-friendly
At the intersection of Route 308 in the middle of town, this historic site got its start in 1766 and still retains its cellar-like lobby where dusty travelers once rested in front of a crackling fire in the days of stagecoach travel. The rooms in the original inn are exquisite, with big cozy beds and roomy bathrooms. The newer, inexpensive motel rooms are often referred to as the 'kennel' because pets tend to be vocal and odiferous guests.

WHISTLEWOOD FARM B&B
☎ 845-876-6838; www.whistlewood.com; 52 Pells Rd, 3 miles from Rhinebeck; weekday $150-250, weekend $180-295; pet-friendly; 📖
Sitting on a hill that enjoys the expansive sky and the whistling wind, this combination B&B and horse stable is on 40 acres of land with walking trails frequented by foxes and other country critters. Evocative of big-sky country, Whistlewood is decorated with a Western country motif. There are standard rooms in the main farmhouse, some with shared bath, and one garden room with its own entrance and bath. A heavily laden table of baked goods is always available for in-between snacking, a sun-porch can consume slow-starting mornings and satellite TV provides crucial access to SportsCenter. In a separate carriage house, two conjoined units share a comfortable common space and kitchenette.

EATING

RHINEBECK DELI
☎ 845-876-3614; 112 E Market St; mains $3-10; ⏱7am-5pm
In the morning, the so-called town criers assemble around the simple tables for coffee and the leisurely life of retirement. The younger set

clamors around the deli counter for takeaway sandwiches and meals before scurrying off to work.

CALICO RESTAURANT & PATISSERIE

☎ 845-876-2749; 6384 Mill St/Rte 9; mains $4-15; ⏰8am-8:30pm Wed-Sat, 8am-4pm Sun

This little tea room has the best pastries in a town that likes pastries. The menu has expanded to include French-inspired bistro fare.

CRIPPLE CREEK RESTAURANT

☎ 845-876-4355; 22 Garden St; mains $18-25; ⏰5-9pm Mon & Wed-Sun, later on weekends

In a town where every sandwich-slinger is a CIA graduate, a restaurant has to qualify the chef's credentials. This restaurant, serving eclectic American cuisine, receives the honor of being a certain CIA professor's favorite restaurant for special events. In a characterless office park, the restaurant has a long bar, classical music and impressive artwork (check out the Chagall on the wall).

SANTE FE RESTAURANT

☎ 845-757-4100; 52 Broadway/Rte 78, Tivoli; ⏰5-10pm Tue-Sun

With outdoor seating to watch the sun bid adieu and a funky dining room, Sante Fe is informal, but the food is inventive. A menu of nuevo Mexican cuisine will burst any preconceptions that 'nuevo Mexican' was a food writer's joke. The pulled pork taco is a sultry mix of spicy and sweet, and the salsa imparts an earnest burn.

ON THE ROAD: ROUTE 103 TO ROUTE 9G

From Rhinebeck's main intersection, take Route 308 toward Rhinecliff and, before you reach the train station, take a right on to the River Road (Route 103) through sleepy countryside. Just a half-mile past the junction with Route 199 is **Poet's Walk** (Map 6; River Rd/Route 103, Red Hook; admission free; ⏰9am-dusk), a 120-acre park with 2 miles of walking trails that lead through open meadows and along river vistas. The path was originally a road used to haul shipments from the river to higher land. Strolling its course, Washington Irving and other poets found inspiration from its contemplative beauty, so do modern visitors. No vehicles or bikes are allowed.

Follow Route 103 north to the intersection with Route 199. This will lead you east to **Red Hook**, a small community that pops up among the winding roads and green fields, about 5 miles north of Rhinebeck. With hardware stores and pizza parlors, it is more functional than Rhinebeck, its showpiece neighbor. Stop in for a bite at the **Historic Village Diner** (Map 6; ☎ 845-758-6232; 39 N Broadway, Red Hook; mains $10-15; ⏰6am-9pm), parked in a converted railcar. Perky coeds man the counter, and folks either

DETOUR: BACK ROADS FROM RHINEBECK TO HUDSON

If you're tired of being faithful to Route 9, break off for a bit with a westward swoop through Dutchess County horse country. From Rhinebeck, follow Route 308 west to Route 199 toward Pine Plains. Just outside of this charming town is the junction for Route 82 toward Ancram, which travels right through the heart of undulating pastures with grazing thoroughbreds. Cultivated fields punctuate the horse farms, which together easily outnumber the human population nearby. Route 82 skirts by **Lake Taghkanic** (p38), a state park with a sparkling lake that is mobbed in the summer but a relative castaway on a fall weekday, even during an Indian summer. If you're playing hooky from work, stop by for a quick dip. Follow Route 82 over the **Taconic State Parkway** (p35) for another 8 miles until your reunion with Route 9, which will lead you north into Hudson.

stumble or saunter in, depending on the hour of the day, for hatbox-sized stacks of flapjacks and greasy hamburgers.

Can you squeeze in just a little more historic-house hunting? C'mon, **Montgomery Place** (Map 6; ☎ 845-758-5461; River Rd/Route 103, west of Route 9G, Annandale-on-Hudson; adult/senior/student $7/6/4, grounds pass $3; ⏰10am-5pm Wed-Mon Apr-Oct, call for winter hours) is totally worth it, honest. It's an 1805 Neoclassical riverside villa, but the grounds are among the prettiest of any of the great estates. Designed by the great landscape architect Andrew Jackson Downing, the grounds have all the components of a masterpiece landscape painting: a sweeping lawn, the tranquil Tivoli Bay at its base, trails through hemlock forest, and a framed vista of the indigo Catskill Mountains held in an inverted bowl of gold-streaked clouds. Among the 434 acres there are also rock gardens and a waterfall. In the fall you can pick apples from the orchard and in summer you can reserve a space for lawn games. If you're hooked, backtrack to Route 103 toward the town of Annandale-on-Hudson.

Eventually the River Road (Route 103) turns into Annandale Rd as it passes through the 600-acre campus of **Bard College** (Map 6; www.bard.edu), which was founded in 1860 as a school for men; today it is coed and best known for its devotion to the creative arts. The Frank Gehry–designed **Fisher Center for the Performing Arts** (Map 6; ☎ 845-758-6822) is a recent addition to the campus and hosts opera, music and drama performances, including the acclaimed Bard Music Festival in August.

Take Route 103 to the junction with Route 9G north to Route 78 leading into the little village of **Tivoli**. Part artist colony, part Bard dorm and part rehab center for burned-out urbanites, Tivoli's residents wake up around 3pm, do some errands and then collect around dusk at the **Sante Fe Restaurant** (p29). If you're day-tripping through town, check out the **Tivoli Artists' Co-op** (Map 6; ☎ 845-757-2667; 60 Broadway; admission free; ◷5-9pm Fri, 1-9pm Sat, 12-4pm Sun), a gallery that shows rotating exhibits of local artists' works. This organization also sponsors the annual Tivoli Street Painting Festival in early October.

If you've seen one house museum, you might as well see them all. What if you get back and your friends chastise you for skipping 'the best' one? You see the problem; there is just too much face to lose. So from Tivoli, head west on Route 78 past the small downtown. At the church, hang a right onto Woods Rd, which will take you the back way to **Clermont** (Map 6; ☎ 518-537-4240; 1 Clermont Ave, off Woods Rd; adult/senior/student/child $5/4/4/1; ◷11am-5pm Tue-Sun Apr-Oct, 11am-4pm Sat & Sun Nov-Mar), an early-18th-century home of the Robert Livingston family. Part of the attraction here is the history of the home and its occupants. Born in Scotland, the Livingstons made a fortune in the new nation, and a great grandson, Robert R Livingston, was a delegate to the Continental Congress that produced the Declaration of Independence. He also negotiated the Louisiana Purchase of 1803 from Napoleon for Thomas Jefferson. A consummate overachiever, grandson Livingston is *the* Livingston who became partners with Robert Fulton, who was busy working on a contraption called a steamboat. In 1807 the first steamboat, *North River,* made its appearance on the Hudson. Later, it was called *Clermont.*

The house is Georgian in style, and original furnishings are on view. The grounds, which extend down to the river, offer a fine view of the Catskill Mountains across the river. The fragrant lilacs and linden trees are major draws when they bloom. The house is best visited in early evening as the setting sun swathes the scene in celestial colors.

HUDSON

Population 7500; Map 7

Hudson is a decompression zone for Manhattanites looking for a dose of extracurricular activity without having to travel too far into the bush. Only a two-hour train ride away from New York City, Hudson's once struggling downtown artery, Warren St, is now crowded with blocks of antique stores selling everything from charming junk to the family jewels. South of Warren, stately townhouses, centered around the courthouse, are where the first families of Hudson displayed their fortunes from the town's thriving whaling industry. Hudson's other claim to fame is its (former) red-light district, said to be the first in the country. Despite the downtown's recent makeover, in its core Hudson is still an unemployed factory town, and a downtrodden neighborhood just a block north of Warren St creates an incongruous picture with Warren's antique stores and Soho-style bistros.

Hudson River School of Landscape Painters

Big soaring skies and little hamlets: both the majestic and the ordinary were captured by the Hudson River School, a group of landscape painters who made the rural Hudson Valley and the wilderness of the Catskill Mountains an important subject of American art. The expansion and prosperity that came in the first decades of the 19th century – especially after the completion of the Erie Canal in 1825 – gave the country a strong national consciousness and, along with it, the freedom to begin exploring distinctly American (that is, non-European) themes. The new artists shunned popular historical themes along with formal portraiture in favor of depicting everyday life – romanticized to be sure, but with a detailed realism that was new to the American art scene around New York. Like Washington Irving, author of *The Legend of Sleepy Hollow*, the romantic impulse was at work.

Thomas Doughty was the self-taught founder of the school, but its leading spirit was Thomas Cole, who was followed by Asher Durand, John Kensett and Frederic Edwin Church (who turned his home at Olana into a 'real' landscape painting). Both Cole and Church injected allegorical elements into their work, but most members of the school worked using a purely representational style, one which some critics found to be uninspired and tedious.

The school did succeed in elevating the status of landscape painting in the US and in immortalizing the mountain slopes, valleys, streams and falls of the region. Even John James Audobon's famous *Birds of America* bears the influence of the school's detailed recording of nature.

Today, a bright day in the Hudson Valley is sure to bring out a few painters to sit by a quiet riverbank or budding hillside with brush in hand and eye on the same landscapes that inspired their famous predecessors. Although on a cloudy day when the sky is moody, it is easier to behold the dramatic lighting represented on the canvases of the Hudson River school.

SIGHTS & ACTIVITIES

AMERICAN MUSEUM OF FIREFIGHTING

☎ 518-822-1875; 117 Harry Howard Ave; admission free; ⏰9am-4:30pm

A homegrown attraction, this museum honors New York's proud volunteer fire-fighting tradition with displays of 84 fire engines from man-powered carts to engine-powered machines. The oldest fire engine in the collection was built in 1725 and used by Hudson Company No 1. A gooseneck engine from 1811 still bears the battle scars it earned fighting New York City's Great Fire of 1835. The museum docents are happy to explain the history of the equipment, which isn't particularly well signed. A small but touching memorial to the firefighters who lost their lives on September 11, 2001 is the most recent addition.

OLANA

☎ 518-828-0135; Rte 9G; adult/senior/child $7/5/2; ⏰11am-5pm Tue-Sun Apr-Oct, call for winter hours

Olana was the home of landscape painter Frederic Edwin Church

(1826–1900), one of the earliest American painters to receive celebrity status. With his fortunes from the sales of his most famous works, *Niagara* (1857) and Heart of the Andes (1859), Church set out to create a three-dimensional landscape painting using a small rise overlooking the Hudson River as a canvas. This very same hill was used by Church as a sketching spot when he was a student of Thomas Cole, who lived across the river in Catskills. Church originally planned to build a French chateau on the land he bought in the mid-19th century. But after a two-year trip to the Middle East, he commissioned Calvert Vaux to assist in the technical details for a villa with influences of Moorish architecture, which was finished in the late 1870s.

True to the aesthetic movement, Church mixed religions, cultures and materials. The house is built like a typical Middle Eastern home around a central corridor, but the wings form a symmetrical cross. Huge picture-glass windows look out at the Hudson River, an unobstructed view in Church's time now marred by an industrial factory.

Despite modernity at the doorstep, the house and grounds are breathtaking. With carriage trails diving into thick forests and emerging into meadow vistas, Church commented that he 'can make more and better landscapes in this way than by tampering with canvas and paint in the studio.' No argument could be made that the view from the 'front porch' on a summer afternoon resembles some of the large canvases of the Hudson River school of landscape painters.

In addition to house and landscape tours, Olana hosts lecture series throughout the year on such topics as Victorian gardens, floral hybrids and cottage gardening. A summer arts camp for children ages 6-12 occurs in mid-July and early August.

Olana is about 5 miles south of Hudson on Route 9G. From downtown Hudson, go south on S 3rd St, which turns into Route 23/9G. Stay on 9G heading south (away from the Rip Van Winkle Bridge). Look for the sign on the left and go up the hill.

SLEEPING & EATING

ST CHARLES HOTEL
☎ 518-822-9900; 16-18 Park Pl; d $100, includes breakfast
This stout, local standby is right on the village green and has several floors of predictable rooms with all the standard amenities.

HUDSON CITY B&B
☎ 518-822-8044; 326 Allen St; d $130-170, includes breakfast
Kenneth Jacobs, proprietor of the former 1850s mayor's home, offers six tastefully decorated bedrooms in an historic 1865 townhouse. The house itself is a history and architecture lesson, as is the surrounding neighborhood, which was built by the successful shipping magnates of the 1800s.

COLUMBIA DINER
☎ 518-828-1310; 717 Warren St; mains $6-10
This shiny chrome diner has soothing 1970s colors of fuchsia and

beige along with perky waitstaff and Greek lunch classics, like stuffed cabbage and peppers.

WUNDERBAR & BISTRO

☎ 518-828-055; 744 Warren St; mains $8-14; 🕙11:30am-2pm & 5pm-10pm Mon-Fri, 5-10pm Sat

Hudson doesn't have much in the way of indigenous cuisine; instead it borrows liberally from the restaurant culture of New York City. One of many chic bistros that line Warren St, Wunderbar breaks out from the pack with a reasonable lunch special. The menu is straightforward American, like roasted chicken with fries and pork roast with mashed potatoes, and the portions stay true to the American mantra of 'big is beautiful.'

ON THE ROAD: ROUTE 9

Beyond Hudson are miles of undisturbed country lanes that wind around shady creek beds, vista hillocks and gnarled apple orchards. Roads aren't well signed or predictable, so buy a Jimapco Columbia County map to navigate like a champ. From Hudson, take Route 9 toward **Kinderhook**, an old Dutch village and home of the **Martin Van Buren National Historic Site** (Lindenwald; ☎ 518-758-9689; Rte 9H; $3; 🕙9am-4pm Mon-Fri). The eighth US president, Martin Van Buren was born in Kinderhook and later retired to this site, a sedate Federal-style house with 90 acres of forested walking trails. The tour of the house is an informative introduction to this forgotten president, the first born as a US citizen. Serving under Andrew Jackson and then as chief from 1837 to 1841, Van Buren was against the expansion of slavery into the new territories and subsequently lost to William Harrison, who rallied under the famous 'Tippecanoe and Tyler too' slogan. Van Buren later made another unsuccessful bid for the White House; in Virginia, he won only nine votes inciting a local critic to remark, 'We're still looking for the son-of-a-bitch who voted nine times.'

From here you can weave your way through tiny hamlets to the **Shaker Museum & Library** (p39).

If returning to Hudson from Lindenwald, a series of itty-bitty country lanes provide a more scenic alternative to Route 9. From the Van Buren Site, take a right onto Route 9H to Route 25 (Albany Ave). At the first major intersection, turn left heading south down Route 25 (which is now called Hudson Ave) toward Stockport. Keep an eye out for Route 22, which will be on your right-hand side as you head into the village, and turn right; Route 22 follows the Stockport Creek back to Route 9. The route might seem like a wild goose chase, but isn't that the fun of backroads?

TACONIC STATE PARKWAY

Strung out along a high ridge in the western Hudson River Valley near the Berkshire Mountains, the Taconic State Parkway extends for 105 miles from the Bronx River Parkway north to Albany and provides a scenic yet expedited route from New York City to the Catskills and the Adirondacks. This isn't merely a modern highway that coincidentally passes through noteworthy scenery. Following in the river valley's aesthetic traditions, the parkway complements the landscape of rugged mountains and sweeping vistas with a country lane–width of asphalt tied to state parks. North of Bear Mountain Parkway, the Taconic dons its most charming aspect: an unhurried route that crests hills as if launching into the fleecy clouds and then dips into lush valleys of glistening and dynamic greens. Exit ramps dump travelers right into the lap of farmland and wilderness, seemingly continents away from the density of the city.

First envisioned in the 1920s by the proposed parkway's commissioner, Franklin D Roosevelt (if you haven't signed onto the FDR cult yet, it is time to join), the parkway almost died on the drawing board after fierce budget debates with a competing plan on Long Island, which was backed and (ultimately outmaneuvered the Taconic) by civic planner Robert Moses. The Taconic wasn't completed in its entirety until the 1960s.

ON THE ROAD: TO DUTCHESS COUNTY

From its southern mouth, the parkway efficiently bisects busy Westchester County as a fast-moving thoroughfare decorated with majestic oaks and rustic stone overpasses more charming than the utilitarian modern highways. Around the Peekskill area, the parkway gains altitude through the rounded hills of the Hudson Highlands and starts to slip out of civilization.

A portion of the Appalachian Trail (AT) knits through the 7000-acre **Clarence Fahnestock Memorial State Park** (☎ 845-225-7207; Rte 301, Carmel; admission free; open year-round), east of Cold Spring. Local hikers do the 8-mile portion of the AT here or concentrate on the wildflowers along the Three Lakes Trail in early summer. Another popular hike is through the abandoned mining town of Dennytown on the Catfish Loop Trail. Mountain bikers come for the wide, open trails with steady climbs and the joy of solitude. The park is also known for its winter park, a favorite of cross-country skiers. Camping (☎ 800-456-2667; www.reserveamerica.com; tent $13) is also available.

North of Fahnestock Park, the parkway eases into the rolling hills of Dutchess County's horse country with expansive views and picturesque farms dotting the landscape.

Fall Color

The last gasp of the growing season urges people into the wilderness with an almost religious intensity. Heeding the invitation to witness nature's cyclical demise, people traipse through the woods to be immersed in a towering garden of intense rusts, reds, yellows and pinks, and to inhale the crisp air scented by wet leaves and distant woodstoves.

The Hudson Valley shares in this great autumnal performance, and people debate endlessly about where to find the best fall color. Their experience has more to do with timing than with location, as almost any vantage point, country road or hiking trail will fit the bill if caught at the right moment. And so begins the art of watching the trees, both a scientific and back-porch pursuit. 'Spotters' or 'leaf-peepers' (fall-foliage watchers) recommend heading out when there is still enough green in the mix to add depth and contrast to the tapestry. This will also ensure that there will still be color if a heavy storm barges through at the last minute. Beware of 'show offs,' which are young trees that turn several weeks before the pack.

For updates on fall color, call ☎ 800-354-4595, tune into the Weather Channel, or log onto www.foliagenetwork.com.

MILLBROOK

Population 1400; Map 5

This area has long been an upscale alternative to the Hamptons on Long Island and effortlessly exudes a privileged, old-money feel. It's a maze of backroad retreats, and riding trails and genteel country homes seem to appear and disappear among the winding country roads. Nearby Route 22, which runs north-south near the Connecticut and Massachusetts borders, is also one of the state's most bucolic corridors, dotted with farms and pastures, antique stores and blue-plate family diners.

Millbrook itself is as pretty a little town as you'll find, complete with a village green, shiny fire station and spiffy Main St diner. This is a town with a center, and it's an easy place to linger. The area counts among its more famous visitors one Timothy Leary, who spent some of his early LSD-experimenting days around Millbrook at the nearby Hitchcock estate. Some of the townsfolk were scandalized, but it's hard to tell these days if they're complaining or if they're bragging.

SIGHTS & ACTIVITIES

INNISFREE GARDEN

☎ 845-677-8000; 362 Tyrell Rd; weekday/weekend $3/4; ⏰10am-4pm Wed-Fri May-Oct, 11am-5pm Sat & Sun

This garden is one of the most beautiful in the valley – and there are many gardens here. When the great Irish poet William Butler Yeats wrote 'The Lake Isle of Innisfree,' he described a spot in the imagination that is always alive. The 200-acre garden here was designed by Walter Beck, who designed a series of cup gardens with terraces, streams and stones arranged in meticulous fashion, all of which comes to a delicate rest on the edge of Tyrell Lake. It's all reminiscent of Yeats' 1893 poem, part of which reads: 'And I shall have some peace there, for peace comes dropping slow/ Dropping from the veils of the morning to where the cricket sings…'

To find Innisfree from Millbrook, head west on Route 44 at the traffic light, turn left on Tyrell Rd and follow the signs.

INSTITUTE OF ECOSYSTEM STUDIES
IES; ☎ 845-677-5359; ☻ecology shop 11am-5pm Mon-Fri, 9am-5pm Sat, 1-5pm Sun, greenhouse closes 3:30pm

This center for the study of ecology is between the Taconic and the town of Millbrook, just off Route 44A where a sign will point the way. The institute is a combination arboretum, gardening-education and wetland-ecology center. In addition to being a lovely spot to walk through, the center offers courses that last from one day or weekend to a week or six weeks. Courses include Natural Science Illustrating and Drawing in the Greenhouse. There are also canoe excursion trips to study wetland ecology, as well as other trips. Call for more information or write for a brochure: Institute of Ecosystem Studies, Box R, Millbrook, NY 12545.

SLEEPING & EATING

COTTONWOOD MOTEL
☎ 845-677-3283; Rte 44; d weekday $89-110, weekend $115-155

Just outside town, this sparkling white motel is set back from the road so that the din of traffic doesn't echo into your room. The rooms are suburban splendor, and some have outdoor patios.

CAT IN YOUR LAP B&B
☎ 845-677-3051; Old Rte 82 at the Monument; d $75-125; pet-friendly

This farmhouse offers two bedrooms in the main house and barn suites with fireplace and kitchenette. Bill Berensmann, the co-proprietor, is an architect by training and can give you great tips on appreciating the Hudson Valley architecture.

MILLBROOK DINER
☎ 845-677-5319; 3266 Franklin Ave/Rte 44; mains $4-10; ☻6am-9pm

Near the village green, this town landmark has basic diner fare of eggs and waffles. The diner's old wooden figurehead is reputedly the prettiest lady in town (but don't spread this around). The tables inside are adorned with jukebox units, and the food – especially breakfast – is just right.

ALLYN'S RESTAURANT & CAFÉ
☎ 845-677-5888; 4258 Rte 44; mains $15-22; ☻11:30am-9:30pm Mon, Wed & Thu, 11:30am-10:30pm Fri & Sat, 11:30am-3pm Sun

About 4 miles east of Millbrook, this equestrian-themed restaurant offers excellent daily soups, a nice selection of local wines and a variety of dishes reflecting a Continental-Asian fusion.

ON THE ROAD: DOING THE CHATHAMS

Continuing north, the parkway fetches a faint outline of the sleeping Catskills to the west and sleepy country valleys to the east. Just two hours from New York City, **Lake Taghkanic State Park** (Map 1; ☎ 518-851-3631; 1528 Rte 82, Ancram, 1 mile south of Rte 82 and the Taconic; $6 per car; open year-round) surrounds a crystal blue lake free of motorized vessels and is popular with local families. Of the lake's two sandy beaches, the one on the west end is worth staking out a spot early on a busy summer weekend. In the fall, the park is still beautiful and pleasantly deserted. Camping and cabins are available in pretty wooded lots across the road from the lake. If you can get reservations for the rustic cottages on the south side of the lake, you'll be in for a secluded retreat. Contact **ReserveAmerica** (☎ 800-456-2267; www.reserveamerica.com; tent $13, cabin $190-370 per week) for lodging reservations.

Return to the Taconic and drive north through lovely countryside

---

DETOUR: DUTCHESS COUNTY WINE COUNTRY

While Hudson Valley's wines will never unseat a French vintage, exploring the Dutchess County 'wine trail' is a good excuse for a country drive. Often characterized as beginner wines (more sweet than dry), the region's drinkable products are cultivated in a landscape similar to that of the veritable Rhine Valley; however, New York's harsh winters relegate the industry to hardier varieties, especially fruit wines. For a brochure on the Dutchess County vineyards, visit www.dutchesswinetrail.com.

One of the prettiest drives is to the rustic outpost of **Clinton Vineyards** (☎ 845-266-5372; Schultzville Rd, Clinton Corners; ⏰11am-5pm Fri-Mon), with a low-key tasting room offering a view of the vineyard beyond. From the Taconic Parkway at the Salt Point Turnpike exit, head east through Clinton Corners, then left on Schultzville Rd; the winery is 3 miles from the parkway. It's known for its Seyval Blanc and does a decent sparkling wine. Stop by for the fall harvest to see the sweat and dirt that goes into this elegant product.

Put your designated driver in charge and strike out for **Wing's Castle** (⏰tours 12-5pm Wed-Sun Jun-Aug, 12-5pm Sat & Sun Sep-Oct), a private residence made out of found objects to create a grand, recycled castle. From the Taconic's Salt Point Turnpike exit, head south on Route 13 (Clinton Corners Rd) to Route 82 north. Turn left onto Shunpike Rd (Route 57) and continue just past Millbrook Winery to Bangall Rd, where you'll turn left. The castle will be at the top of the hill on the left.

The Shakers

One of the many sects to follow the trail of New England religious migration, the United Society of Believers in Christ's Second Appearing came from England with Mother Ann Lee in 1774. More popularly known as the Shakers, this movement believed that it was God's intention for men and women to live separately but equally. Mother Ann's particular interpretation of the world came after several miscarriages. She was thrown in jail for her preachings, and while there she claimed that she became the second incarnation of Jesus Christ in female form. In her new role, she experienced visions urging her and her followers to go to America. The most prominent Shaker community was centered in New Lebanon, New York, near the Massachusetts state line, in 1792.

The Shakers got their nickname from their love of music and dance, all in the name of religious ritual and harvest celebration. The moniker took hold as word spread of their excited religious services in which members often shook with emotion when seized with the Holy Spirit. The Shakers also had the unique ability to simultaneously entertain the notions of communal living and celibacy. During its heyday, New Lebanon was a self-sufficient community of 600 Shakers, and other establishments were founded throughout the country. Relying on new converts and adopted orphans, the Shakers maintained active communities until the 20th century. With declining populations, the New Lebanon families sold their property to consolidate with other Shaker communities in 1947.

The **Shaker Museum & Library** (below) started out as the personal collection of John S Williams. More than 80% of the collection traces back to New Lebanon, and the present site is housed in Williams' own converted barn in Old Chatham. Recently the museum received a grant to purchase relevant sites in New Lebanon and is planning to build a 50,000-sq-ft museum within the massive ruins of the great stone barn. A timeline of these changes has yet to be announced, so if you're in the area, it is a good idea to call ahead.

to the **Chathams**, a group of quiet small towns where the biggest event is the annual **Columbia County Fair** (www.columbiafair.com), held each Labor Day weekend. The chief attraction here is the **Shaker Museum & Library** (Map 8; ☎518-794-9100; www.shaker museumandlibrary.org; 88 Shaker Museum Rd, Old Chatham; adult/senior/child $8/6/4; ☺10am-5pm Mon & Wed-Sun May-Oct), which provides a rustic yet educational view of this ascetic communal sect, now known mostly for their simple, beautiful furniture. The museum is about 2 miles from the Taconic, or 20 miles from the town of Hudson via Route 66.

Down the street from the Shaker Museum is the maker of a locally famous cheese, the **Old Chatham Sheepherding Company** (Map 8; ☎888-743-3760; www.blacksheepcheese.com, 155 Shaker Museum Rd, Old Chatham; ☺9am-5pm). It welcomes visitors to its 600-acre farm, the largest sheep dairy farm in the country. More than 1200 Friesland dairy sheep nibble on young tufts of grass amongst the rolling hills in this picture-perfect spot. Visitors can watch the milking and production process; bring along a cooler so you can stock up on fresh yogurt, ricotta and Hudson Valley Camembert.

Backtracking to Route 13 back to Chatham Center, head out on Route 66 toward Chatham (why all the Chathams?) to eat lunch at **Chatham Bakery & Coffee Shoppe** (Map 8; ☎ 518-392-3411; 1 Church St at Rte 66; mains $6-8; ⏱10am-9am). The corner coffee shop makes the nakedest burger you'll ever meet: known as the Wallyburger, it's greasy grilled meat slapped between two pillows of white bread. In the fall, you'll find pumpkin donuts. With a full belly, you can either hop onto the Taconic or take Route 66 to **Hudson** (p31).

WESTERN BANK

Temperament and topography differ on the western side of the Hudson River from the more refined eastern bank. The towns are scruffier and less manicured, with fewer intellectual attractions. The weekend holidaymakers of the Gilded Age chose the eastern bank because of the easy access to the train, and the western bank was left wild so that the wealthy could enjoy an unmarred view. State parks and preserves abound, affording hiking and outdoor opportunities within the metaphoric stone's throw from New York City. For country and hippiedom, the western bank claims the disparate attractions of West Point (home to the US Military Academy) and Woodstock (a counterculture darling).

Embarking on a west-bank rendezvous, Manhattanites should jump across the Hudson River at the George Washington Bridge and follow the scenic Palisades Parkway north to river-hugging Route 9W, straight into compact Nyack.

NYACK

Population 6700; Map 1

Nyack sits across the river from Tarrytown. A ferry once connected the towns, but now the towering Tappan Zee Bridge almost overshadows this former manufacturing and boat-building center. Of late, Nyack is a quaint commuter village of New York City. A vibrant arts scene has flourished in and around Nyack, and five times a year the main streets are closed off to host street fairs. The downtown is a pleasant stroll with bookshops and small restaurants.

Edward Hopper House Art Center (☎ 845-358-0774; 82 N Broadway; $1; 🕙1-5pm Thu-Sun) occupies the childhood home and tells the life story of the American painter who so hauntingly captured loneliness and melancholy. **Pickwick Bookshop** (☎ 845-358-9126; 8 S Broadway; 🕙10am-7pm Mon-Fri, 11am-6pm Sat & Sun) has a rumpled air and a sprawling corner for children's books. You can easily lose track of time here, as the owner himself does. **Ben Franklin Bookshop** (☎ 845-358-0440; 17 N Broadway; 🕙11am-5: 30pm Mon-Fri, 11am-6:30pm Sat & Sun) has a good selection of local history and literature, but the specialty is rare mystery and science fiction.

Skylark Café (☎ 845-358-7988; 84 Main St; mains $6; 🕙7am-10pm) is a combination coffee shop and bar that combines the fixtures of every town under own roof. In the mornings the elders sip coffee alongside the winos choking down medicine beers. The food is really negligible compared to the local characters.

O'Donoghue's (☎ 845-358-0180; 66 Main St; mains $5-7; 🕙11am-11pm, kitchen closed Mon) is an Irish pub-restaurant serving as an informal community center; if you need a plumber or an apartment, many residents recommend stopping in at OD's. And if you're hungry, the lunch specials get rave reviews.

ON THE ROAD: PALISADES PARKWAY

Heading north on the Palisades Parkway shoots you right into the heart of the Hudson Highlands, whose graceful peaks form a deep cavern on either side of the river linked by the silver necklace of the Bear Mountain Bridge. Reflecting the vertical heights around it, the river plunges to its deepest point through this passage. You can explore the highlands at **Harriman State Park** (Map 1; ☎ 845-786-5003; Palisades Parkway btw exits 16 & 17; ☼8am-6pm Memorial Day–Labor Day; parking $6-8), which has several well-maintained hiking trails and three lakes for paddling and swimming. **Bear Mountain State Park** (Map 1; ☎ 845-786-2701; parking $6; open year-round) borders the western bank of the Hudson River and was once the designated spot for Sing Sing Prison, until President Teddy Roosevelt intervened in 1910. After the prison proposal was defeated, Union Pacific railroad president EW Harriman organized the properties' formation into a state park. The view from Bear Mountain's peak (1305ft) takes in the Manhattan skyline on a clear day as well as the river and surrounding mountain greenery. **Camping** and **cabins** (☎ 800-456-2267; tent $13, cabin $190-370 per week) are available at Harriman, and lodges and hotel rooms are available in **Bear Mountain Inn** (☎ 845-786-2731; fax 845-786-0862; d $90-100), at the foot of Bear Mountain.

WEST POINT

Population 7100; Map 9

Dedicated to duty, honor and country, when viewed from across the river, the **US Military Academy at West Point** looks as if its castle-like turrets jutting out of the landscape in irregular and imposing tiers had been carved prehistorically from the rocky shore. Before an academy was established here, West Point was a key fortification during the Revolutionary War. Sometime between 1778 and 1780 a massive wrought-iron chain (with a log-boom to protect it) was stretched across the river to Constitution Island to prevent British ships from attempting to control river navigation. In 1802 the military academy, the oldest of its kind in the nation, was founded. Notable graduates include famous military heroes, astronauts and presidents.

The campus is impressive. Miles of pathways crisscross a grand preserve of redbrick and gray-stone Gothic- and Federal-style campus buildings, churches, temples and stadiums, as well as a boat landing and panoramic views of the Hudson River. The military presence. is tireless even in the landscaping; anything hinting at disorder has been neatly trimmed. Just walking around can make you yearn for a haircut. You might even imagine the plight of a young Edgar Allan Poe, a cadet in 1830, who was dismissed for insubordination after only eight months of less-than-military endeavor.

The visitor entrance for the campus is in the village of Highland Falls, which reflects the rather blue-collar aesthetic of a military operation, with just a touch of New England. Here you'll find the **West Point Visitors Center** (☎ 845-938-2638; www.usma.edu; 2107 N South Post Rd; ✆9am-4:45pm), about 100 yards south of the military academy's Thayer Gate. Behind the visitors center is the **West Point Museum** (admission free; ✆10:30am-4:15pm), which

Bookworm Vacation

Unleash your repressed bookworm on a Hudson Valley ramble. It's the birthplace of great leaders, writers and historical events – who could resist devouring every book ever written on the place? Plus, the area is filled with used bookstores to further aggravate your paperback addiction. Here are a few titles to keep an eye out for:

- **World's End** (1987), by TC Boyle, follows burnout Walter Van Brunt's recurring 'accident' with history in his hometown of Peterskill (artistic veil for Peekskill). Reminiscent of Gore Vidal, Boyle manages to convey heaps of historical information through despicable characters doing deplorable things that keep you glued to the book.
- **The Hudson** (1939), by Carl Carmer, offers short vignettes on historical and cultural aspects of the Hudson Valley. This book achieved almost sacred status in the 1960s, when it was used to prove the artistic and aesthetic merits of the valley during the contentious debates on the proposed construction of a power plant on top of Storm King Mountain. (Incidentally the plant was defeated, and Storm King Mountain offers one of the most beautiful drives in the valley.)

Look for them at one of these local independent bookstores:

- **Alternative Books** ☎ 845-331-5439
  35 N Front St, Kingston
- **Ariel Booksellers** ☎ 845-255-8041
  3 Plattekill Ave, New Paltz
- **Ben Franklin Bookshop** ☎ 845-358-0440
  17 N Broadway, Nyack
- **Bruised Apple** ☎ 914-734-7000
  923 Central Ave, Peekskill
- **Golden Notebook** ☎ 845-679-8000
  29 Tinker St, Woodstock
- **Hope Farm Press** ☎ 845-246-3522
  252 Main St, Saugerties
- **Second Story Book Shop** ☎ 914-238-4463
  75 North Greeley Ave, Chappaqua

traces the history of warfare, famous generals and historical weapons in addition to West Point history.

For a glimpse of the cadets' strict military life and a tour of the campus, you must join an organized bus tour. This is a post–September 11 security procedure and is subject to change based on alert-levels issued by the federal government. **West Point Tours** (☎ 845-446-4724; http://westpointtours.com; adult/child $7/4; 1-hour tours 9:45am-3:30pm Mon-Sat, 11:15am-3:30pm Sun, no tours Sat during football season) operates the tours from a kiosk inside the visitors center. Photo identification is required for all visitors. Bus tours take in the following campus sites: Cadet Chapel, Post Cemetery, Michie Stadium, the Plain (where George Washington drilled the American forces) and other battle monuments.

SLEEPING & EATING

Expect rates for all hotels to increase greatly during graduation and other West Point–related events.

HOTEL THAYER
☎ 845-446-4731; inside Thayer Gate; d high season $240-260, low season from $120; 🖳

This five-story Gothic-style hotel stands sentry at West Point's entrance gate and looks as if it is the command center of the entire campus. Inside, a spit-polished military ambience prevails. Odd-numbered rooms claim a view of the Hudson River, while even-numbered rooms look out over the parade grounds. To enter and leave the campus, guests of the hotel must pass through security checkpoints where machine-gun–clad guards inspect the driver and passengers' IDs and car. It is unnerving until the guards flash their innocent 18-year-old smiles.

WEST POINT MOTEL
☎ 888-349-6788; 156 Main St; d $74-125; 🖳

The closest lodging to campus, this independent motel has standard-issue rooms.

ANDY'S RESTAURANT
☎ 845-446-8736; 281 Main St; mains $5-12; 🕔5:30am-7pm

Tucked into the squat downtown business district, Andy's gets the morning coffee drinkers, lunchtime work crews and the dinnertime bachelors. To the metallic ringing of the fry cook's spatula, diners feast on Americana specials: stuffed peppers, eggs any style and baked chicken.

ON THE ROAD: ROUTE 218

As you're heading out of Highland Falls, make a right on to Route 218 north. The road makes the steep ascent of **Storm King Mountain**, chasing through fog banks and out onto rocky bluffs with the ribbon-like sweep of the river below. Squat stone walls belt cars into the sharp S-curves. The descent lands in the shady village of **Cornwall-on-Hudson**. To scope out more of this lovely scenery, head to the **Museum of the Hudson Highlands** (☎ 845-534-5506; www.hudsonhighlands.org; $2; ☾10am-4pm Thu-Sat), a nature and art center set deep in a damp forest. As Route 218 heads into town, at the Village Restaurant (which will be on your right), turn left onto Payson Rd. A companion site, Kendridge Farm, is located just a mile away on Route 9W and has a farmhouse, barn, wildflower meadow, labyrinth and wetland trails.

While you're in this neck of the woods, don't miss the fantastic **Storm King Art Center** (Map 1; ☎ 845-534-3115; www.stormking.org; Old Pleasant Hill Rd, Mountainville; adult/senior/student $9/7/5; ☾11am-5:30pm Wed-Sun Apr-Nov), an outdoor walk-through sculpture park featuring some of the finest modern and contemporary sculpture in North America, including works by modern masters Calder, Moore and Noguchi. The setting matches the artwork, angle for angle. Guided walking tours and shuttle-bus tours are also available. To get to Storm King Art Center from Cornwall-on-Hudson, follow Route 218 to the traffic circle in the center of town; take the Quaker Ave spur to the first stoplight and then follow the signs.

North of Cornwall, **Newburgh**, a former whaling center, is a textbook example of American architecture from the Revolutionary War period to the present. Unfortunately, one chapter of that same textbook would include the demise of such historical towns. The oldest of Newburgh's remaining commercial and residential buildings are in disrepair, and the best views are looking east across the river. History buffs might be able to stomach a visit to this crippled city in order to see **Washington's Headquarters State Historic Site** (☎ 845-562-1195; cnr Washington & Liberty Sts; adult/child $4/1; ☾10am-5pm Mon, 10am-5pm Wed-Sat, 11am-5pm Sun mid-Apr–Oct), the home of a small museum where Washington stayed from 1782–83; he was there until the end of the Revolutionary War. The site features several galleries, period furniture and a 50-foot map that wraps around an entire room.

Hop onto I-87 (the New York State Thruway) north of Newburgh as Route 9W crashes into junkyards and industrial wasteland.

NEW PALTZ

Population 6000; Map 10

This crunchy college town (home of the State University of New York/SUNY-New Paltz) is filled with lovestruck couples, thrift-store fashionistas and mountaineering junkies. Funky shops and pizza-and-beer joints line the cramped main road into town. While downtown is historic and charming, most people come here to play in the butte-like Shawangunk (aka 'Gunks') Mountains that loom in the distance. For guides to the Gunks and other reading material, stop by **Ariel Booksellers** (☎ 845-255-8041; 3 Plattekill Ave).

SIGHTS & ACTIVITIES

HISTORIC HUGUENOT STREET
☎ 845-255-1889 visitors center; 6 Broadhead Ave; adult/child $8/3; ⊙9am-5pm Tue-Sun May-Oct

In 1677 French Huguenots founded New Paltz after they were forced out of Europe. Proof of the town's founding families can be found along this preserved street, which claims to be the oldest in the country. Seven stone buildings survive (or have been reconstructed) and are open to the public through guided 1½ hour tours. The street is preserved by a historical society consisting of descendants of the settling families.

MINNEWASKA STATE PARK
☎ 845-255-0752; $7 per car; ⊙dawn-dusk; day use only, no camping

Popular with rock climbers, this huge state park also offers cross-country skiing (groomed trails), snowshoeing, biking (40 miles of trails), hiking, picnicking and summer swimming. Take Route 299 west to Route 44/55 and go west for 4 miles to the marked entrance. If you need gear or technical assistance, visit **High Angle Adventures** (☎ 845-658-9811, 800-777-2546; www.highangle.com; 178 Hardenburgh Rd, Ulster Park); the staff also leads full-day climbing courses.

WALLKILL VALLEY RAIL TRAIL
A converted rail line now provides a 12-mile bike route from New Paltz to Rosendale and Gardiner to Shawangunk. For a trail map, visit the Wallkill Valley Rail Trail Association's website (www.gorailtrail.com). The entrance to the trail from New Paltz is one block from **The Bicycle Rack** (☎ 845-255-1770; 13 N Front Street), a bike shop that can provide advice on riding this and other trails around New Paltz.

SLEEPING & EATING

NEW PALTZ HOSTEL
☎ 845-255-6676; www.newpaltzhostel.com; 145 Main St; dm/d $22/57

For clean, cheap accommodations in a communal setting, you can't beat the cheery New Paltz Hostel. The walls are filled with artwork, the owners are friendly, and there is a kitchen for preparing meals.

MINNEWASKA LODGE
☎ 845-255-1110; www.minnewaskalodge.com; Rte 44/55, just east of Rte 299; d $155-189

These contemporary hotel rooms are a bit staid, but the location is beautiful and the grounds immaculate. Each room has a balcony that captures mountain views.

MOHONK MOUNTAIN HOUSE
☎ 845-255-1000, 800-772-6646; www.mohonk.com; 1000 Mountain Rest Rd, off Rte 6, north of New Paltz; s/d from $215/358

Reminiscent of California's lavish Hearst Castle, this Victorian resort, a National Historic Landmark, is worth visiting even if you're not looking to stay the night. Alongside a stunning blue lake, the resort offers children's activities, hiking trails and a museum. Some rooms have a balcony and/or fireplace.

BACCHUS BAR & GRILLE
☎ 845-255-8636; 4 S Chestnut St; lunch $6-10, dinner $13-18; ⏰11am-2am Mon-Fri, 10am-1am Sat & Sun

Touted as one of the city's best restaurants, Bacchus' real claim to fame is its massive beer selection – last count, 300 from all over the world. (Welcome to a college town where the food runs a distant second to drinking.) Before you become a liquid globetrotter, dig into a plate of Southwest-inspired dishes or an arty pizza. Food service stops at 10pm.

McGILLICUDDY'S RESTAURANT & TAP HOUSE
☎ 845-256-9289; 84 Main St; mains $6-13; ⏰11am-4am

This is a cozy pub big enough to welcome families with kids in tow as well as raucous college students. The portions are all-American sized and include everything from sandwiches to fajitas to steaks. Fans rave about the Irish potato soup, and the black and tans are poured by expert hands.

ON THE ROAD:
ROUTE 6 TO ROUTE 32

Leaving New Paltz by its western exit via Route 299, cross over the steel-ribbed bridge and take the first right onto Mountain Rest Rd through a wide valley. At the first fork in the road, veer left onto Route 6/Mohonk Rd and make the climb up the massive table-top Mohonk Mountain. Near the plateau is the turnoff for the **Mohonk Mountain House** (p46), a century-old resort enveloped in several thousand acres of protected land known as the **Mohonk Preserve** (Map 1; ☎845-255-0243; www.mohonkpreserve.org; weekend/weekday $8/6; ⏰dawn-dusk). Hiking and carriage trails crisscross the grounds, which are well loved by cross-country skiers and leisure hikers. Two miles from the visitors center is the Sky Top tower, which claims a view of six states on a clear day.

Continuing on Route 6, the road makes a descent worthy of a symphony. A graceful C-loop spirals the rim of the bowl-shaped valley crowded with bowing cornfields and a succession of violet mountains cascading in the distance. If caught near sunset, the cloud-streaked sky imparts a celestial glow to the landscape. Eventually Route 6 runs into the town of High Falls, home of the **Delaware & Hudson Canal Historical Society Museum** (D&H Canal Museum; ☎845-687-9311; Mohonk Rd; adult/child $3/1; ⏰11am-5pm Thu-Mon, 1-5pm Sun May-Oct). The canal was built in the 1820s to link the Hudson River with the coal fields of Pennsylvania. Today five locks remain and can be visited via a leisurely walk from the road. Heading east on Route 213 to Route 32 north will deliver you to Kingston.

KINGSTON

Population 23,450; Map 11

Of the big industrial towns along the Hudson River, Kingston has, in a small package, all the elements of a *real* city. A scenic walkable downtown, stuffy suits, thuggish high-school kids, hard-working but marginalized immigrants and unkempt artists are all rolled up together with a dash of urban grittiness. This diversity makes the city seem more alive than the pickled historic districts of postcard-worthy towns elsewhere along the valley.

SIGHTS & ACTIVITIES

STOCKADE DISTRICT

Filled with sedate stone buildings, many of which have been converted into shops and restaurants, this district dates back to the 17th century. In 1777, the first New York State Senate met briefly at the **Senate House State Historic Site** (☎ 845-338-2786; 296 Fair St; adult/child $4/1; ☻10am-5pm Mon-Sat, 1-5pm Sun Apr 15–Oct 30), built circa 1635, when the British drove the governing body from New York City. The **Old Dutch Church & Cemetery** (☎ 845-334-9355; 272 Wall St) is quiet and shady, and the tombstones date back to the 1700s. New York's first governor, George Clinton, is buried here. The reformed Protestant Dutch church (1695) has services on Sundays. George Washington visited the church in 1782, and his visit is memorialized in a plaque on the church's exterior wall.

A modern-day historic worshipping spot is **Alternative Books** (☎ 845-331-5439; 35 N Front St; ☻10:30am-5pm), filled with shelves of used books concentrating mainly on the arts and humanities. This is a good spot to inquire about the art scene in the area or to pick up a copy of the literary journal *Heliotrope,* which is published in the Hudson Valley.

RONDOUT HISTORIC DISTRICT

Once a bustling 19th-century terminal port of the Delaware and Hudson Canal, the Rondout today is a revived neighborhood and shopping area, boasting bars and seafood restaurants.

Within the historic district, the **Trolley Museum of New York** (☎ 845-331-3399; www.tmny.org; 89 E Strand St; adult/child $3/2; ☻12-5pm Sat & Sun late May–mid-Oct) offers rides on old trolleys and has static displays of trolley, subway and rapid-transit cars from the US and Europe.

River life is celebrated at the **Hudson River Maritime Museum** (☎ 845-338-0071; 50 Rondout Landing; adult/child $10/8; ☻11am-5pm May-Oct). The museum's gallery has displays of all types of boats. After you've had your fill looking at ships, hop on one for a 15-minute ride on the Rondout Creek to the Hudson River, where you can check out the 1913 Rondout lighthouse.

KINGSTON'S ART GALLERIES

Artsy refugees from overpriced Manhattan and San Francisco have found a comforting oasis in Kingston. As a result, galleries and art happenings have proliferated throughout town. The first Saturday of every month, the galleries stay open late and invite the public to meet the artists. The city also hosts an annual sculpture exposition in the summer and fall. Visit the Arts Society of Kingston's website (www.askforarts.org) for a gallery guide.

A few noteworthy galleries include **The Gallery at Deep Listening Space** (☎ 845-338-5984; 75 Broadway; ☼1-4pm Sat & Sun). Funded through the Pauline Oliveros foundation, the gallery introduces people to Deep Listening, an experimental movement dealing with resonance, reverberation and long tones to invoke a listening meditation.

Watermark/Cargo Gallery (☎ 845-338-8623; 111 Abeel St; ☼3-9pm Thu & Fri, 1-9pm Sat, 1-5pm Sun) has museum-quality African art and artifacts as well as rotating exhibits by contemporary artists.

SLEEPING & EATING

THE BLACK LION MANSION B&B
☎ 845-338-0410; www.theblacklionmansion.com; 124 W Chestnut St; d from $100

All the rooms in this late 19th-century mansion are decorated differently, and all are stunning. The grand old house has giant windows, sweeping staircases and amazing views of the surrounding mountains.

ADELE'S RONDOUT B&B
☎ 845-331-8144; 88 W Chester St; d from $115

This classy Federal-style home is airy and decorated in warm colors with lots of rugs and a large broad porch. The four rooms are well appointed, and the owner has a wealth of information about the area.

KINGSTON COOKS
☎ 845-338-2959; 307 Wall St; mains $2-6; ☼7am-6pm Mon-Fri

This favorite Stockade lunch spot serves cheap health-conscious food. There is a large selection of sandwiches, fresh salads and smoothies. You can eat in or take the food away.

JANE'S HOMEMADE ICE CREAM
☎ 845-338-8315; 305 Wall St; mains $2-7; ☼10am-6pm Mon-Fri; 11am-4pm Sat, closed Sun

Next door to Kingston Cooks, Jane's is not just about ice cream (although the frozen treat is quite tasty). It also has a large selection of low-fat wraps and Mexican selections. The place even advertises that it has a Weight Watchers specialist around to help design meals.

EL DANZANTE

☎ 845-331-7070; 720 Broadway; mains $5-10; ⏱10am-10pm

While you wait for your food at this Mexican restaurant, you can overhear the cook singing along with the melodramatic ballads of lost love and shrill trumpets. The taco al pastor (marinated pork) is delicious and comes wrapped in white paper to resemble little horns of spicy plenty.

DOWNTOWN CAFÉ BAR & GARDEN

☎ 845-331-5904; 1 W Strand St; lunch mains $8-12, dinner mains $13-24; ⏱10am-3pm & 6-10pm Mon-Fri, 5:30-11pm Sat, 9pm-9am Sun

In the Rondout District, this breezy bistro is filled with sparkling glasses of water, citrus colors and the smells of simmering pots of stew and freshly brewed coffee. Graziano Tecchio, the Italian chef decked out in denim overalls, creates magical dishes of complementary flavors. Deep-fried soft-shell crab with lime cilantro and grilled asparagus, Sardinian pasta with eggplant ragout, and wild salmon with stone-ground mustard are some of the seasonal dishes. Local and organic produce are used when available, and interesting vegetarian items also make an appearance.

ENTERTAINMENT & SHOPPING

THE UPTOWN

☎ 845-339-8440; www.uptowngathering.com; 33 N Front St

This is an intimate club that draws big-name jazz musicians from New York City as well as eclectic performances like bluegrass jammers or literary readers. This space is run by the proprietor of **Alternative Books** (p48), next door.

ARTIE'S

☎ 845-338-9659; 44 N Front St; ⏱24hr

A local dive, Artie's never closes its doors and serves a no-nonsense draft beer, cold and refreshing. Members of the art-pop band Mercury Rev are said to stop in for a swill.

ZABORSKI EMPORIUM

☎ 845-338-6465; 27 Hoffman St; ⏱11am-5pm Wed-Sat, 1-5pm Sun

Gleaners and antique pirates could get lost for days in this architectural salvage warehouse of four floors and 60,000 sq ft. Narrow footpaths ramble through rooms stuffed with claw-foot tubs, antique doors, WWII memorabilia, books, light fixtures and other survivors predating the 1970s. If you're looking to get rid of used stuff, Zaborski also buys contents of houses and attics.

WOODSTOCK

Population 6200; Map 12

Best known for the 1960s event that didn't actually happen here, Woodstock feels like an unmade bed – comfortable but disheveled.

The lush mountain landscape acts like a spring for counterculture thinking, and the aura of the hippie days is still alive and well, even in the younger generation, who rap about energy fields while standing in line at the local health-food store. More than just a center of free-love nostalgia, Woodstock is a legitimate arts colony dating back to the early 1900s. Artists, craftspeople, musicians and appreciators have been filing through town ever since. One of the best displays of Woodstock's artistic endeavors is its many summer and fall festivals. In September the **Woodstock Film Festival** (☎ 845-679-4265; www.woodstockfilmfestival.com) takes place over three days and draws movie aficionados and Hollywood celebrities to town.

SIGHTS & ACTIVITIES

DOWNTOWN WOODSTOCK

Seeing Woodstock means strolling about town, enjoying the friendly feel of the place, and browsing through the locally owned shops. Woodstock's main drags, Tinker St and Mill Hill Rd, are at the heart of the action, and the small village green offers the perfect vantage point for people-watching. If you happen to be in town on Christmas Eve you'll be one of the first to know how Santa Claus arrives on the green. This is

Spiritual Retreats

Just as a casual observer, you'll notice the rejuvenating effects of the Hudson River Valley. Its dense, mysterious woods inspire silent reflection that is often drowned out in everyday life. To drink a full draught of this intangible, consider visiting one of the valley's many retreat centers:

- **Chuang Yen Monastery** (☎ 845-225-1819; www.baus.org; 2020 Rte 301, Carmel; closed winter) contains one of the largest Buddhist statues in the Western Hemisphere and also offers Sunday morning meditation sessions followed by a vegetarian lunch.
- **Graymoor Spiritual Life Center** (☎ 845-424-3671; www.atonementfriars.org; Rte 9, Garrison), situated on a small mountain in the Hudson Highlands, is run by the Franciscan Friars and Sisters of Atonement, who offer weekend ecumenical retreats for married couples, nature lovers and those interested in alcohol recovery.
- **Karma Triyana Dharmachakra** (see listing, p53)
- **Omega Institute for Holistic Studies** (☎ 845-266-4444, 800-944-1001; www.eomega.org; 150 Lake Dr, Rhinebeck) is a popular retreat center located on 140 lakefront acres and offers workshops on holistic health, yoga, transformational psychology and meditation
- **Zen Mountain Monastery** (☎ 845-688-2228; www.mro.org; S Plank Rd, Mt Tremper), in the Catskill Mountains, offers Zen training, meditation instruction, retreats and chanting services..

the best-kept secret around, and it's never dull; Santa's been known to travel by camel and hang-glider – on separate occasions, of course.

The Golden Notebook (☎ 845-679-8000; www.goldennotebook.com; 29 Tinker St; ☺10:30am-7pm daily) is an excellent bookstore with a helpful staff knowledgeable about local attractions. Next door is a children's store, which has a selection of children's books on tape.

Castaways (☎ 845-679-3459; 36 Mill Hill Rd) has lots of resale men's and women's fashions, including brand names. They also sell new jewelry and accessories.

About midway through town you'll find the **Center for Photography** (☎ 845-679-9957; www.cpw.org; 59 Tinker St; admission free; ☺12-5pm Wed-Sun). This attractive and serious gallery offers contemporary and historical exhibits, lectures and photography workshops year-round. It's well worth checking out.

Woodstock Artists' Association (☎ 845-679-2940; 28 Tinker St; ☺12-5pm Tue & Wed) shows rotating exhibits of local artists' works. One of the oldest art associations in America, the Woodstock Artists' Association collaborated with the Depression-era Works Progress Administration (WPA) to document the history and artistry of the Catskills.

Peace & Music: The Woodstock Festival

About half a million people descended on Max Yasgur's farm in Bethel, New York (40 miles southeast of the town of Woodstock), from August 15 to 17, 1969, for a music festival billed as 'Three Days of Peace & Music.' The lineup of musicians for the Woodstock Festival – Joan Baez; Joe Cocker & the Grease Band; Country Joe & the Fish; Crosby, Stills & Nash; Arlo Guthrie; Richie Havens; Jimi Hendrix; Santana; John Sebastian; Sha Na Na; Sly & the Family Stone; Ten Years After; and The Who – has never been matched.

Festival promoters sold tickets for a remarkable $7 for one day and $18 for three days. The entire event cost only $3 million to stage; unfortunately, less than one quarter of the half-million concertgoers paid for admission, and the festival had trouble paying its bills.

Despite numerous setbacks ranging from broken toilets to a serious mud problem after a day of rain (earning the festival its 'Hog Farm' nickname), there were no riots and no violence. It was the most successful hippie gathering in the world. The most violent scene probably occurred when activist Abbie Hoffman ran on stage to make a speech, only to be greeted by The Who's Pete Townshend, who promptly bashed him over the head with his electric guitar. Lucky he didn't run into Jimi Hendrix, who often set his guitar on fire.

Alan Gerry, a native to the area and a pioneer in the cable-TV industry, purchased the original Woodstock site in 1996. He landscaped the festival grounds and added a parking lot. Plans are underway for a $40-million performing arts center that will showcase both classical and popular music. The center is slated to open in late 2004 or early 2005.

BYRDCLIFFE ARTS COLONY & THEATER

☎ 845-679-2079; www.woodstockguild.org; Upper Byrdcliffe Rd

This is what transformed Woodstock from a quarrying and farming town into a magnet for generations of artists. Englishman Ralph Radcliffe Whitehead founded the complex in 1902 and invited weavers, metal workers and potters to join his community of artisans. In the spirit of the Arts and Crafts movement, Whitehead's colony was a reaction against the mass-factory production of the industrial revolution. The artists who answered the 'ad' for craftspeople to teach at this new art school also impressed their trade and tradition on the town itself, and created a legacy of artistic expression that survives today.

The 1930s folk movement and their 1960s descendents often met here to share their common vision of peace and justice. Their hopeful message was set to music by songwriters and performers, including Pete Seeger; Peter, Paul & Mary; Louisiana bluesman Leadbelly; and Bob Dylan. Ashcan artist George Bellows (1882–1925) spent his summers here, as did actor Chevy Chase when he was a child accompanying his artist parents.

Today the colony hosts residencies, craft demonstrations, exhibitions and performances at the Byrdcliffe Theater and other surviving Arts and Crafts–style buildings on the 300-acre site. Performances are announced in the *New York Times* and the local *Woodstock Times.* If you arrive when an event isn't scheduled, the grounds are open to the public, and self-guided maps are available from the theater. To get there, take Rock City Rd north from the village green to the Glasco Turnpike, head west to Upper Byrdcliffe Rd, then turn right and head north to the colony.

KARMA TRIYANA DHARMACHAKRA & OVERLOOK MOUNTAIN

Map 13; ☎ 845-679-5906; 352 Meads Mountain Rd

Karma Triyana Dharmachakra is a popular Buddhist center and Tibetan monastery that regularly offers teachings ranging from the introductory to the advanced. Meditation instruction is available by appointment free of charge. Meditation retreats and lectures are also offered year-round.

Spectacular views of the surrounding countryside and the Hudson River can be found at the top of **Overlook Mountain**. The 2.4-mile trail starts at the parking lot across from the monastery. To reach the monastery from town, drive up Rock City Rd for about 2 miles and look for the signs.

SLEEPING

TWIN GABLES GUEST HOUSE

☎ 845-679-9479; 73 Tinker St; d from $64

This quirky 1930s-style house opens it doors to budget-minded visitors. With tons of character, Twin Gables has nine guest rooms, each decorated in a different color scheme with matching walls, floors and bedspreads. A superb location, it is located right in the center of town, spitting distance from Woodstock's easygoing energy.

WOODSTOCK INN ON THE MILLSTREAM
☎ 845-679-8211; 38 Tannery Brook Rd; d $107

Tidy white walls and clean rooms are standard at this motel. Quiet and small, it's a three-minute walk from downtown. Each room comes with its own porch, perfect for passing a warm afternoon.

BED BY THE STREAM
Map 13; ☎ 845-246-2979; www.bedbythestream.com; Rte 212; d from $79; ▣

Located in a quiet wooded setting alongside a stream, this barn-like inn has swimming (of both the *au naturel* and chlorinated varieties) and is close to hiking and skiing trails. Private and shared bath accommodations are available.

SAUGERTIES-WOODSTOCK KOA
Map 13; ☎ 845-246-4089; Rte 212; sites $30, cabins $55-79; ☯Apr-Nov

About halfway between Woodstock and Saugerties, this friendly KOA has shady wooded sites and small munchkin-sized cabins. From this stargazing vantage point, you are also an easy drive from one of Woodstock's best restaurants, **New World Home Cooking Co** (p55).

EATING

LANDAU GRILLE
☎ 845-679-8937; 13 Tinker St; mains $8-20; ☯11:30am-9:30pm Mon-Fri, later on weekends

You may have to wait a while to get a table here, but the food is worth the wait. Sit outside and try one of the well presented and fresh pasta dishes.

JOSHUA'S
☎ 845-679-5533; 51 Tinker St; breakfast $6-8, mains $12-16

Breakfast is served until 3pm, and there are countless dishes to choose from. For an almost unprecedented convergence, order flapjacks alongside one of Joshua's Middle Eastern dishes, like hummus, babaganoush and tabouli. Why hasn't McDonald's created such a culinary convention?

BREAD ALONE
☎ 845-679-2108; 22 Mill Hill Rd; mains $2-5; ☯7am-6pm Sun-Thu, 7am-7pm Fri & Sat

This is a Catskills chain and a landmark for bread lovers. Since most folks cannot live by bread alone, the shop also offers fine pastries, morning burritos and eggs, fresh salads and several gourmet deli items.

ENTERTAINMENT

Gone is the Tinker Street Cafe, where Bob Dylan often played during the early 1960s, but Woodstock continues to be home to a thriving arts and music scene.

TINKER ST CINEMA
☎ 845-679-6608; Tinker St

Films at the Woodstock Film Festival are screened here. Other times of the year, this cinema features the best in recent and classic international and independent film, with an occasional nod to a commercial movie. The theater is on Tinker St on the way out of town, heading towards Bearsville.

BEARSVILLE THEATER
Map 13; ☎ 845-679-2100; Rte 212, Bearsville

This venue puts on plays, concerts and stand-up comedy acts. The theater is next to the restaurants Little Bear and The Bear.

MAVERICK CONCERTS
Map 13; ☎ 845-679-7558; Maverick Rd off Rte 375

Dating back to 1916, this is the oldest chamber music series in the US. Sunday concerts with top performers take place at 3pm from mid-June to early September. Concerts are listed in the Sunday *New York Times*; people often drive up from the city for these.

Dining Beyond Woodstock

There are several excellent restaurants just a short drive from Woodstock. Just 2 miles west of the village green on Route 212 is the small town of Bearsville, is where you'll find the **Bear Café** (☎ 845-679-5555; Bearsville Theater Complex; mains $20), serving American and French bistro fare in a rather serene brookside setting. The food is excellent and popular with local and New York City celebrities.

The adjacent **Little Bear** (☎ 845-679-8899; Bearsville Theater Complex; mains $6-12), which shares the forest setting with the Bear Café, has a well-deserved reputation for serving the best Chinese food north of New York City. The menu offers a few Thai dishes too. In the summer sit outside by the creek. In the winter try the enclosed porch – there's still a creek view.

Hip country gourmet can be found at the **New World Home Cooking Co** (☎ 845-246-0900; Route 212; mains $16-20; ⏲5-11pm daily), halfway between Woodstock and Saugerties. The 'slow-food' eatery specializes in a Caribbean-Thai-downhome mix; Jamaican jerk chicken is a local favorite, along with *ropa vieja* (Cuban pot roast). Big servings in deep-dish plates are the order of the day.

ON THE ROAD: ROUTE 212 TO ROUTE 32

If Woodstock wasn't kooky enough for you, this next stop will convince you that the Catskills might be in communiqué with aliens. **Opus 40** (Map 13; ☎ 845-246-3400; www.opus40.org; adult/child $6/3; ⏰12-5pm Fri-Sun Jun-Sep), built out of an old bluestone quarry, was the life work of creator Harvey Fite, who meticulously carved and set the bluestone into circular pathways and plunging pools that sprawl over 6-1/2 acres and lead somewhat unintentionally to a central monolith. The effect is utterly disturbing, retaining the eerie quality of a forgotten mine where the earth was literally striped away and replaced by a strange religious ruin of unyielding material. Wandering over the pathways and searching for the structure's meaning leads to a mental adventure, conjuring memories of exploring abandoned spaces as a child. Within the complex is the **Quarryman's Museum**, which displays many of Fite's tools arranged as dramatically as the stones he fit together.

To get to Opus 40, take Route 212 heading east of Woodstock towards Saugerties. When you see the Blue Mountain Bistro, turn right on to Route 32 (Glasco Turnpike) and go 3 miles. Look for a big yellow arrow that encourages you to veer right; this is where you will ignore the sign and veer left onto High Woods Rd and then take another left on to Fite Rd.

SAUGERTIES

Population 5000

Quaint and charming, Saugerties was the Hudson River Valley's antiquing capital until it was superceded by the town of Hudson. The narrow Main St is lined with historic redbrick buildings, and fine dining makes it a worthwhile destination if based in Woodstock. Saugerties also hosts a little-known but impressive jazz festival in September, leaning more toward Latin than bebop thanks to upstate-native Alex Torres and his band, Los Reyes Latinos.

For an earful on local politics or for browsing on regional history, stop into the bookstore **Hope Farm Press** (☎ 845-246-3522; 252 Main St; ⏰10am-6pm Mon-Sat).

Another draw is the **Saugerties Lighthouse B&B** (☎ 845-247-0656; www.saugertieslighthouse.com; d low/high season $116/135), single-handedly the most scenic and quirky accommodations in the valley. This 1867 stone lighthouse sits on a manmade base like a gigantic buoy anchored in the brackish Hudson River. The 900-step (1/2-mile) walk from the parking lot to the lighthouse rambles through a small nature preserve subject to flooding during high tide (time your arrival accordingly). The two 2nd-floor bedrooms have experienced little modernization from the lighthouse-keeping days. The rooms are bare bones with shared bath and heated by coal stoves, but the view from the square windows provides an additional sleeping companion – the Hudson River. Meals are served family-style in the cramped kitchen outfitted with a Depression-era fridge and stove. Bring a good book, leave the computer and cell phone behind, and set up camp on the sunny deck for an unhurried vacation. Children are welcome (with an additional charge).

Housed in an 1864 tavern with plenty of outdoor seating, **Café Tamayo** (☎ 845-246-9371; 89 Partition St; mains $15-20; ☸ 6-10pm Thu-Sun) serves new American cuisine and is the petite nucleus of Saugerties' social circles.

If you know when you'll be in town, sign up a week in advance for famous Thursday martini nights ($5 for top-shelf ingredients) at **Chowhound Café's** (☎ 845-246-5158; 112 Partition St; mains $15-22; ☸Wed-Sun). Live music and an international menu also earn Chowhound a slot as a locals' favorite.

Dutch Tavern (☎ 845-246-0073; 253 Main St; mains $7-10; ☸10am-midnight, kitchen closed Mon) was once the haunt of the old-timers but has recently been adopted by a younger generation. Who could resist the petite wooden benches and Dutch knickknacks decorating the walls? Plus a draft of their homebrew, Clogger Lager, allows visitors to toast the region's Dutch heritage.

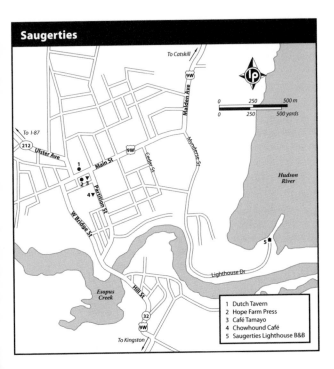

ON THE ROAD: ROUTE 32 TO ROUTE 23A

Although Saugerties and environs flirt with the renowned scenery of the Catskill Mountains, a short drive west will deliver you to the northeast corner of the Catskill Preserve for a majestic sight: the **Kaaterskill Falls**. Well recorded by the Valley's painters, including Thomas Cole, the falls measures in with a 260-foot drop, the highest in New York (compared to Niagara Falls' diminutive descent of 167 feet) and actually makes two plunges on Spruce Creek.

Take Route 212/32 west from Saugerties and turn right onto Route 32 heading north. Turn left onto Route 23A through the town of Palenville, and continue for about 4 miles to the base of the falls. Head up the hill and around the curve to a small parking area on the left. Park here, cross the highway and walk east along the north shoulder for a quarter mile to the trailhead. The rocky and slightly steep trail travels a half mile from the highway to the falls. Since this is a popular hike, you should arrive early on weekends.

To view the top of the falls, continue on Route 23A into the village of Haines Falls and turn right onto North Lake Rd (County Route 18) until you reach Laurel House Rd, where you'll make a right turn. Follow the road to the end, where a trail plunges into the woods.

You can backtrack via Route 23A to Catskill.

CATSKILL

Population 4400; Map 1

History and beauty mingle in the tiny town of Catskill, on the banks of the Hudson River at the mouth of Catskill Creek. Home of Hudson River School painter Thomas Cole in the 19th century, Catskill also played an important role supplying booze during prohibition. Catskill applejack was brewed in the hills surrounding town, and the rough terrain made for good hiding, both for moonshine and gangsters, when the law rolled in. As a result Catskill became a favorite haunt of New York City thugs Legs Diamond and Vincent Coll. Catskill is just across the river from **Hudson** (p31) via the Rip Van Winkle Bridge.

Thomas Cole House (☎ 518-731-6490; 218 Spring St; $4; ⏰10am-4pm Fri & Sat, 1-5pm Sun Jun-Aug), a sober Federal-style residence, has been recently renovated and features exhibits on Cole and his family, including a few of his paintings as well as displays on other Hudson River artists. Large and airy, the yellow and white house overlooks the Hudson River.

Started in the 1930s as a conservation project to protect rare and endangered animals, both tame and wild, from around the world, the **Catskill Game Farm** (☎ 518-678-9595; adult/child $16/13; ⏱10am-6pm Jun-Aug) has remained popular over the decades. The family-operated complex is a zoo that tends to approximately 2000 animals and runs a successful nursery that breeds wild horses from Mongolia. Children will love the large petting zoo, where you can wander amongst tame deer. You can also feed the baby pigs and little lambs by bottle in the farm's nursery. The farm is on Route 32, just outside of town. Follow the signs.

INDEX

See also separate indexes for Eating (p63) and Sleeping (p64).

EATING

SLEEPING